PICCOLO FINGERING CHARTS
Scales & Songs

ISBN: 978-1-969068-06-5
© 2025 The Martin Freres Company, Merimax, LLC
All Rights Reserved

Kimber Books

Thank you!

Thank you for choosing Piccolo Fingering Charts, Scales & Songs. This book is designed for the Piccolo (Key of C) and serves as a clear, dependable reference for beginners and developing players.

Inside, you'll find fingering charts, scales, and familiar songs arranged to make learning both visual and musical. We begin with basic tutorials and gradually introduce more advanced concepts. Once you have the fundamentals down, you can jump to any section you like, and there is no required order.

Some scales and songs are easy and approachable, while others reach beyond the beginner piccolo range and may take more time to master. This book is meant to grow with you, serving as both an introduction and a lasting reference as your skills expand.

Each song includes a QR code that links directly to its audio recording. Listening before you play helps you understand how the notes fit together and strengthens your sense of tone, rhythm, and musical phrasing.

We hope this book becomes a steady companion on your musical journey, one you can return to often whether you're playing your first notes or exploring new challenges.

Happy playing!

Martin Freres

the
MARTIN FRERES COMPANY
MartinFreres.net

Let's Begin

Learning to play the piccolo can feel tricky at first, especially when trying to figure out which fingers to use for the notes on the page. That's why this book has fingering charts right below each note. These charts make it much easier to focus on playing instead of guessing. Here's how to use them.

Understand the Fingering Chart
Each note comes with a fingering diagram that shows you exactly which keys to press.
- Black circles mean press this key down.
- White and Gray circles mean don't press this key.

The fingering chart shown here is used for all the scales and songs in this book. On the music staff, the names of the notes are written above the staff to help you know what to play. Under each note, you'll see a fingering diagram that shows you where to put your fingers on the piccolo. This makes it easier to match the notes to the proper finger positions.

Piccolo Fingering

For each note, press only the keys that are solid black.

By using the piccolo fingering charts, you'll learn faster and have more fun playing, now!

**Notes to Play:
Letter above - Note below**

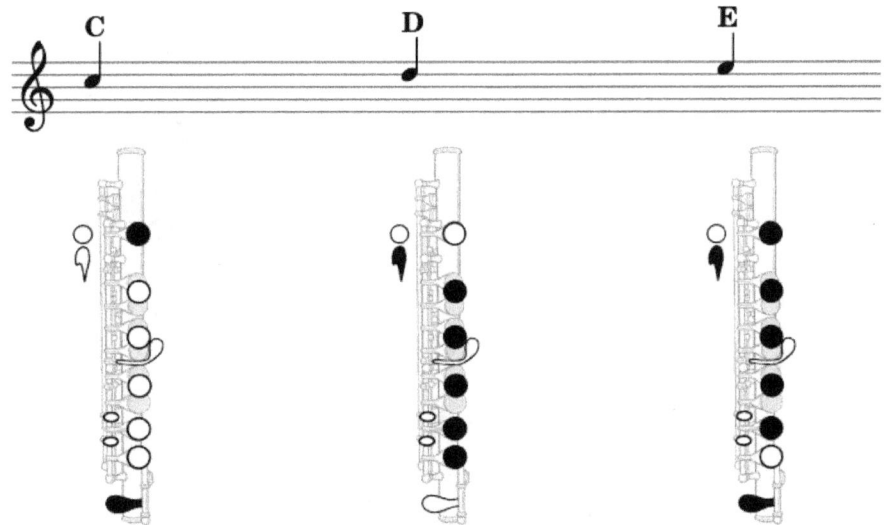

How to Use the QR Codes

Scan the QR code with your phone or tablet camera to hear the song. Listen and play what you hear. QR codes allow you to hear how the notes and rhythm sound together.

Scan the QR Code

to Listen!

Piccolo Fingering
Which Finger Goes Where?

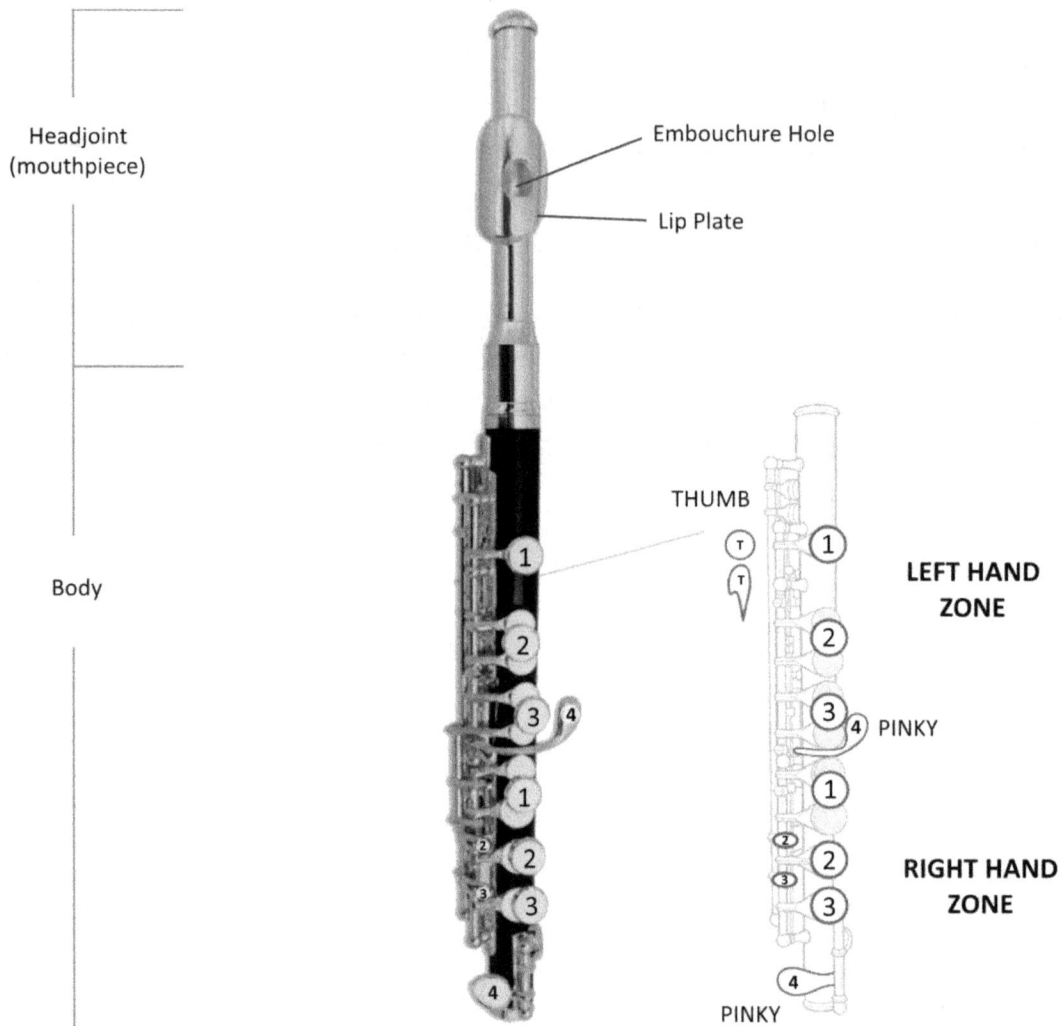

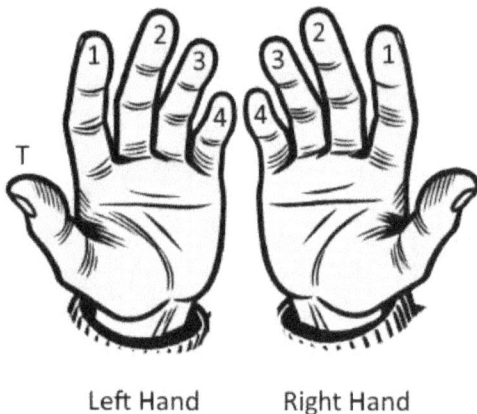

Headjoint
(mouthpiece)

Embouchure Hole

Lip Plate

THUMB

Body

LEFT HAND ZONE

PINKY

RIGHT HAND ZONE

PINKY

1 = Index Finger
2 = Middle Finger
3 = Ring Finger
4 = Pinky Finger

Left Hand   Right Hand

TIP: Start with your left hand on top and your right hand on bottom. Your left-hand thumb supports the instrument and operates the back thumb key.

How to Hold the Piccolo

1. Your Chin Is Your Main Anchor

Start by placing the embouchure hole at the center of your lips, then gently roll the piccolo outward so the lip plate rests beneath your bottom lip. Let the headjoint rest lightly against your chin. This is your main anchor point. The piccolo should feel balanced and secure without being pressed into your face.

2. Your Left Hand Index Finger

Your left-hand index finger helps steady the piccolo. The first knuckle rests lightly against the body of the instrument near the keywork. Its job is not to grip, but to prevent the piccolo from rolling. Keep the finger curved and relaxed so it can easily press left-hand key 1. Think of this finger as a gentle resting point, not a clamp.

3. Your Right Hand Thumb

Your right-hand thumb supports the piccolo from underneath. Place it where it naturally falls when your right-hand fingers hover over the lower keys. Keep the thumb angled slightly upward so it supports the instrument rather than gripping it.

Holding the Piccolo

Your fingers should stay curved and relaxed over the keys, with no tension. Only the fingers needed for the note should press the keys; all others remain relaxed and ready.

The piccolo is supported by three points: the lip plate on the chin, the left-hand index finger, and the right-hand thumb. If the piccolo feels wobbly, check these three support points.

Hold the piccolo slightly downward and to your right. Keep shoulders down, elbows natural, and arms relaxed. The headjoint should remain steady while your fingers move freely. If you feel the need to lift your arms or grip tightly to keep the piccolo stable, one of the support points needs adjustment.

Testing Your Balance

Place the piccolo lip plate on your chin. Position your left index knuckle and your right thumb. Briefly relax your other fingers. If the piccolo remains balanced, your support points are correct. If it rolls or slips, one of the contact points needs adjustment.

Learning to Play the Piccolo

Making a Sound
Making a sound on the piccolo is one of the hardest parts for beginners. Start with just the headjoint (the mouthpiece). *Place the embouchure hole at the center of your lips.* Then roll the headjoint so the hole rolls away from your lips. Let your bottom lip rest on the lip plate, right at the edge of the hole. Leave a tiny space between your lips, like you're quietly saying "boo." Now blow gently across the hole, slightly downward. Once you can get a tone with just the headjoint, assemble the piccolo and try changing how hard you blow and the angle of your air until a clear, steady tone comes out. This takes practice, practice, practice.

Use the Charts While Learning Scales & Songs
When you start playing Scales & Songs, keep using the fingering charts as a guide. Play one note at a time and check your fingers if you need to. After a while, your fingers will begin to remember where to go, and you can follow the music sheet instead of the fingering charts.

Listen for Accuracy
Even if your fingers are in the right spots, your sound might still not be quite right if your breath control or lip positioning (embouchure) isn't right. Use the charts to make sure your fingers are correct, but also focus on creating a clear, steady sound for each note.

Move Away from the Charts
As you get better, challenge yourself to play scales and songs by looking only at the notes on the staff. Let your fingers do the work from memory. The more you practice this way, the more confident and independent you'll become.

Use the Charts When You Need Help
If you're struggling with a note or forgetting a fingering, don't worry, just look at the fingering charts. They're there to help you when you need a quick reminder.

By practicing with these charts and gradually using them less, you'll build strong skills faster and with less frustration. Always remember, the goal is not just to play notes, it's to make music. With time and effort, you'll be playing with confidence and having fun.

Starter C Major Scale

This is the starter C major scale beginning with the note A rather than C. This allows new players to learn a scale before reaching for lower or higher notes that can be tricky to learn. For this version, the notes are: A, B, C, D, E, F, G, then back to A.

For beginners, playing full scales can take time. Some of the lowest and highest notes need more practice, and that is perfectly fine. Play the notes you can, learn them at your own pace, and grow into the rest as you continue.

Each note comes with a fingering diagram showing you which keys to press.
   - Black circles mean press this key down.
   - White and Gray circles mean don't press this key.

Scan the
QR Code

to Listen to
the scale!

C Major Scale (Up)

Practicing the C major scale helps train your ear to hear the sound of a major key, which is important for playing songs and understanding how music fits together. We call it "Up" because the scale begins on the lower C note and moves higher with each new note. This scale is also known as the **C major scale ascending,** and it uses the notes C, D, E, F, G, A, and B. You will find these notes in many of the songs in this book.

For beginners, playing full scales can take time. Some of the lowest and highest notes need more practice, and that is perfectly fine. Play the notes you can, learn them at your own pace, and grow into the rest as you continue.

Many lower and higher notes on the piccolo use the same fingering. To reach the lower or higher sound, adjust your air by using a gentler, downward stream for low notes and a smaller, faster, more focused stream for high notes. Here, the lower C and higher C use the same fingering. Try it!

Each note comes with a fingering diagram showing you which keys to press.
   - Black circles mean press this key down.
   - White and Gray circles mean don't press this key.

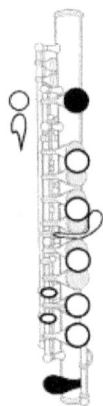

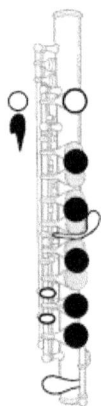

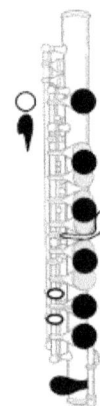

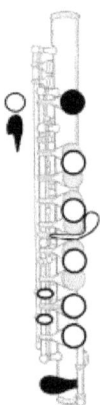

Scan the QR Code

to Listen to the scale!

C Major Scale (Down)

Here is the C major scale going down. We call it "Down" because the scale begins on the higher C note and every new note goes lower in sound. This is also known as the **C major scale descending** and we will play the notes C, B, A, G, F, E, D, then back to C, only lower.

For beginners, playing full scales can take time. Some of the lowest and highest notes need more practice, and that is perfectly fine. Play the notes you can, learn them at your own pace, and grow into the rest as you continue.

Many lower and higher notes on the piccolo use the same fingering. To reach the lower or higher sound, adjust your air by using a gentler, downward stream for low notes and a smaller, faster, more focused stream for high notes. Here, the lower C and higher C use the same fingering. Try it!

Remember, each note comes with a fingering diagram showing you which keys to press.
- Black circles mean press this key down.
- White and Gray circles mean don't press this key.

Scan the QR Code

to Listen to the scale!

G Major Scale (Up)

This is the G major scale ascending. The scale begins on the G note and moves higher in sound with each new note. The G major scale includes the notes G, A, B, C, D, E, and F# (F sharp). The word **sharp** means the note sounds slightly higher in pitch than the regular note, in this case F.

For beginners, playing full scales can take time. Some of the lowest and highest notes need more practice, and that is perfectly fine. Play the notes you can, learn them at your own pace, and grow into the rest as you continue.

Many lower and higher notes on the piccolo use the same fingering. To reach the lower or higher sound, adjust your air by using a gentler, downward stream for low notes and a smaller, faster, more focused stream for high notes. Here, the lower G and higher G use the same fingering. Try it!

Remember, each note comes with a fingering diagram showing you which keys to press.
- Black circles mean press this key down.
- White and Gray circles mean don't press this key.

Scan the
QR Code

to Listen to
the scale!

G Major Scale (Down)

Here is the G major scale descending. The scale begins on the higher G note and every new note goes lower in sound. For the G major scale descending we will play the notes G, F#, E, D, C, B, A, then back to G, only lower.

For beginners, playing full scales can take time. Some of the lowest and highest notes need more practice, and that is perfectly fine. Play the notes you can, learn them at your own pace, and grow into the rest as you continue.

Many lower and higher notes on the piccolo use the same fingering. To reach the lower or higher sound, adjust your air by using a gentler, downward stream for low notes and a smaller, faster, more focused stream for high notes. Here, the lower G and higher G use the same fingering. Try it!

Remember, each note comes with a fingering diagram showing you which keys to press.
   - Black circles mean press this key down.
   - White and Gray circles mean don't press this key.

Scan the QR Code

to Listen to the scale!

F Major Scale (Up)

This is the F major scale ascending. The scale begins on the F note and moves higher in sound with each new note. The F major scale includes the notes F, G, A, B♭ (B flat), C, D, and E. The word **flat** means the note sounds slightly lower in pitch than the regular note, in this case B.

For beginners, playing full scales can take time. Some of the lowest and highest notes need more practice, and that is perfectly fine. Play the notes you can, learn them at your own pace, and grow into the rest as you continue.

Many lower and higher notes on the piccolo use the same fingering. To reach the lower or higher sound, adjust your air by using a gentler, downward stream for low notes and a smaller, faster, more focused stream for high notes. Here, the lower F and higher F use the same fingering. Try it!

Remember, each note comes with a fingering diagram showing you which keys to press.
- Black circles mean press this key down.
- White and Gray circles mean don't press this key.

Scan the QR Code

to Listen to the scale!

F Major Scale (Down)

Here is the F major scale descending. The scale begins on the higher F note and every new note goes lower in sound. For the F major scale descending we will play the notes F, E, D, C, Bb, A, G, then back to F, only lower.

For beginners, playing full scales can take time. Some of the lowest and highest notes need more practice, and that is perfectly fine. Play the notes you can, learn them at your own pace, and grow into the rest as you continue.

Many lower and higher notes on the piccolo use the same fingering. To reach the lower or higher sound, adjust your air by using a gentler, downward stream for low notes and a smaller, faster, more focused stream for high notes. Here, the lower F and higher F use the same fingering. Try it!

Remember, each note comes with a fingering diagram showing you which keys to press.
- Black circles mean press this key down.
- White and Gray circles mean don't press this key.

Scan the QR Code

to Listen to the scale!

D Major Scale (Up)

This is the D major scale ascending. The scale begins on the D note and moves higher in sound with each new note. The D major scale includes the notes D, E, F#, G, A, B, and C#.

For beginners, playing full scales can take time. Some of the lowest and highest notes need more practice, and that is perfectly fine. Play the notes you can, learn them at your own pace, and grow into the rest as you continue.

Many lower and higher notes on the piccolo use the same fingering. To reach the lower or higher sound, adjust your air by using a gentler, downward stream for low notes and a smaller, faster, more focused stream for high notes. Here, the lower D and higher D use the same fingering. Try it!

Remember, each note comes with a fingering diagram showing you which keys to press.
- Black circles mean press this key down.
- White and Gray circles mean don't press this key.

Scan the QR Code to Listen to the scale!

D Major Scale (Down)

Here is the D major scale descending. The scale begins on the higher D note and every new note goes lower in sound. For the D major scale descending we will play the notes D, C#, B, A, G, F#, E, then back to D, only lower.

For beginners, playing full scales can take time. Some of the lowest and highest notes need more practice, and that is perfectly fine. Play the notes you can, learn them at your own pace, and grow into the rest as you continue.

Many lower and higher notes on the piccolo use the same fingering. To reach the lower or higher sound, adjust your air by using a gentler, downward stream for low notes and a smaller, faster, more focused stream for high notes. Here, the lower D and higher D use the same fingering. Try it!

Remember, each note comes with a fingering diagram showing you which keys to press.
- Black circles mean press this key down.
- White and Gray circles mean don't press this key.

Scan the
QR Code

to Listen to
the scale!

B♭ Major Scale (Up)

This is the B♭ major scale ascending. The scale begins on the B♭ note and moves higher in sound with each new note. The B♭ major scale includes the notes B♭, C, D, E♭, F, G, and A.

For beginners, playing full scales can take time. Some of the lowest and highest notes need more practice, and that is perfectly fine. Play the notes you can, learn them at your own pace, and grow into the rest as you continue.

Many lower and higher notes on the piccolo use the same fingering. To reach the lower or higher sound, adjust your air by using a gentler, downward stream for low notes and a smaller, faster, more focused stream for high notes. Here, the lower B♭ and higher B♭ use the same fingering. Try it!

Remember, each note comes with a fingering diagram showing you which keys to press.
- Black circles mean press this key down.
- White and Gray circles mean don't press this key.

Scan the QR Code

to Listen to the scale!

Bb Major Scale (Down)

Here is the Bb major scale descending. The scale begins on the higher Bb note and every new note goes lower in sound. For the Bb major scale descending we will play the notes Bb, A, G, F, Eb, D, C, then back to Bb, only lower.

For beginners, playing full scales can take time. Some of the lowest and highest notes need more practice, and that is perfectly fine. Play the notes you can, learn them at your own pace, and grow into the rest as you continue.

Many lower and higher notes on the piccolo use the same fingering. To reach the lower or higher sound, adjust your air by using a gentler, downward stream for low notes and a smaller, faster, more focused stream for high notes. Here, the lower Bb and higher Bb use the same fingering. Try it!

Remember, each note comes with a fingering diagram showing you which keys to press.
   - Black circles mean press this key down.
   - White and Gray circles mean don't press this key.

Scan the QR Code

to Listen to the scale!

E♭ Major Scale (Up)

This is the E♭ major scale ascending. The scale begins on the E♭ note and moves higher in sound with each new note. The E♭ major scale includes the notes E♭, F, G, A♭, B♭, C, and D.

For beginners, playing full scales can take time. Some of the lowest and highest notes need more practice, and that is perfectly fine. Play the notes you can, learn them at your own pace, and grow into the rest as you continue.

Many lower and higher notes on the piccolo use the same fingering. To reach the lower or higher sound, adjust your air by using a gentler, downward stream for low notes and a smaller, faster, more focused stream for high notes. Here, the lower E♭ and higher E♭ use the same fingering. Try it!

Remember, each note comes with a fingering diagram showing you which keys to press.
- Black circles mean press this key down.
- White and Gray circles mean don't press this key.

Scan the QR Code

to Listen to the scale!

E♭ Major Scale (Down)

Here is the E♭ major scale descending. The scale begins on the higher E♭ note and every new note goes lower in sound. For the E♭ major scale descending we will play the notes E♭, D, C, B♭, A♭, G, F, then back to E♭, only lower.

For beginners, playing full scales can take time. Some of the lowest and highest notes need more practice, and that is perfectly fine. Play the notes you can, learn them at your own pace, and grow into the rest as you continue.

Many lower and higher notes on the piccolo use the same fingering. To reach the lower or higher sound, adjust your air by using a gentler, downward stream for low notes and a smaller, faster, more focused stream for high notes. Here, the lower E♭ and higher E♭ use the same fingering. Try it!

Remember, each note comes with a fingering diagram showing you which keys to press.
- Black circles mean press this key down.
- White and Gray circles mean don't press this key.

Scan the QR Code to Listen to the scale!

What is Your Embouchure?

em·bou·chure | \ ˌäm-bü-ˈshu̇r

Your piccolo embouchure is the way you shape your lips, mouth, and facial muscles to direct the airstream across the tone hole (embouchure hole). It's the main control point for your sound. The angle, firmness, and size of the lip opening all work together to create tone, pitch, and projection.

Small, gentle adjustments work best. Never force the sound. A balanced embouchure helps each note speak clearly and makes playing feel easier.

What Is Embouchure Pressure?
On the piccolo, "pressure" doesn't mean pushing or tightening. Instead, it refers to the gentle firmness of the lips and the focus of the air as it moves across the embouchure hole.

If the balance isn't quite right, the piccolo will tell you:

Too much tension
- Tone becomes tight or sharp
- Notes feel difficult to produce
- Air feels forced rather than flowing

Too little focus
- Sound becomes airy or unfocused
- Notes may not speak immediately
- Tone can feel wide or fuzzy

The goal is a relaxed lip shape with a steady, centered airstream that strikes the edge of the tone hole at the proper angle. Watching yourself in a mirror can help you see and adjust the shape and angle.

Tips to Improve Your Embouchure

Bottom Lip: Rest the lip plate lightly against the center of your bottom lip, covering a small part of the tone hole.

Top Lip: Shape the top lip to angle the air slightly downward. Keep it relaxed, not tight.

Lip Shape: Form a small, focused opening like saying "boo" to direct a steady, centered airstream.

Notes, Beats & How to Count Them

Here's a quick guide to the most common note types and how long each one lasts. In this book, we focus on learning to play by listening to the piece and then playing what you hear. You'll learn more about timing as you continue your musical journey.

Eighth (8th) notes
Each eighth note lasts for half a beat. Use steady air and move quickly to the next note.

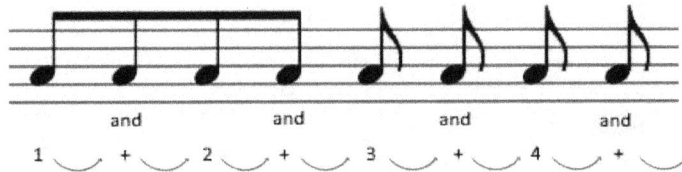

When we see a plus sign: + we say 'and'

Quarter notes
A quarter note lasts 1 full beat. Use steady air and hold each note for one full beat. Each beat lasts the same amount of time.

Half notes
We play each half note for a count of 2 beats. Use steady air and hold each note for a full 2 beats. Each note lasts the same amount of time.

Whole notes
We count each whole note for 4 full beats. Use steady air and hold for 4 beats.

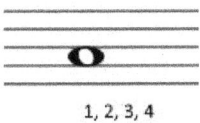

Dotted Quarter notes last for one and a half beats (that's 3 half beats).

How it works

A dot adds a little extra time—half the value of the note it's attached to.

Dotted Half notes each count for 3 beats. Use steady air and hold for 3 beats.

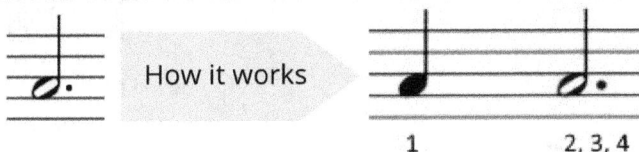

How it works

B Major Scale (Up)

This is the B major scale ascending. The scale begins on the B note and moves higher in sound with each new note. The B major scale includes the notes B, C#, D#, E, F#, G#, and A#.

For beginners, playing full scales can take time. Some of the lowest and highest notes need more practice, and that is perfectly fine. Play the notes you can, learn them at your own pace, and grow into the rest as you continue.

Many lower and higher notes on the piccolo use the same fingering. To reach the lower or higher sound, adjust your air by using a gentler, downward stream for low notes and a smaller, faster, more focused stream for high notes. Here, the lower B and higher B use the same fingering. Try it!

Remember, each note comes with a fingering diagram showing you which keys to press.
- Black circles mean press this key down.
- White and Gray circles mean don't press this key.

Scan the QR Code

to Listen to the scale!

B Major Scale (Down)

Here is the B major scale descending. The scale begins on the higher B note and every new note goes lower in sound. For the B major scale descending we will play the notes B, A#, G#, F#, E, D#, C#, then back to B, only lower.

For beginners, playing full scales can take time. Some of the lowest and highest notes need more practice, and that is perfectly fine. Play the notes you can, learn them at your own pace, and grow into the rest as you continue.

Many lower and higher notes on the piccolo use the same fingering. To reach the lower or higher sound, adjust your air by using a gentler, downward stream for low notes and a smaller, faster, more focused stream for high notes. Here, the lower B and higher B use the same fingering. Try it!

Remember, each note comes with a fingering diagram showing you which keys to press.
   - Black circles mean press this key down.
   - White and Gray circles mean don't press this key.

Scan the QR Code

to Listen to the scale!

E Major Scale (Up)

This is the E major scale ascending. The scale begins on the E note and moves higher in sound with each new note. The E major scale includes the notes E, F#, G#, A, B, C#, and D#.

For beginners, playing full scales can take time. Some of the lowest and highest notes need more practice, and that is perfectly fine. Play the notes you can, learn them at your own pace, and grow into the rest as you continue.

Many lower and higher notes on the piccolo use the same fingering. To reach the lower or higher sound, adjust your air by using a gentler, downward stream for low notes and a smaller, faster, more focused stream for high notes. Here, the lower E and higher E use the same fingering. Try it!

Remember, each note comes with a fingering diagram showing you which keys to press.
- Black circles mean press this key down.
- White and Gray circles mean don't press this key.

Scan the QR Code

to Listen to the scale!

E Major Scale (Down)

Here is the E major scale descending. The scale begins on the higher E note and every new note goes lower in sound. For the E major scale descending we will play the notes E, D#, C#, B, A, G#, F#, then back to E, only lower.

For beginners, playing full scales can take time. Some of the lowest and highest notes need more practice, and that is perfectly fine. Play the notes you can, learn them at your own pace, and grow into the rest as you continue.

Many lower and higher notes on the piccolo use the same fingering. To reach the lower or higher sound, adjust your air by using a gentler, downward stream for low notes and a smaller, faster, more focused stream for high notes. Here, the lower E and higher E use the same fingering. Try it!

Remember, each note comes with a fingering diagram showing you which keys to press.
   - Black circles mean press this key down.
   - White and Gray circles mean don't press this key.

Scan the
QR Code

to Listen to
the scale!

D♭ Major Scale (Up)

This is the D♭ major scale ascending. The scale begins on the D♭ note and moves higher in sound with each new note. The D♭ major scale includes the notes D♭, E♭, F, G♭, A♭, B♭, and C.

For beginners, playing full scales can take time. Some of the lowest and highest notes need more practice, and that is perfectly fine. Play the notes you can, learn them at your own pace, and grow into the rest as you continue.

Many lower and higher notes on the piccolo use the same fingering. To reach the lower or higher sound, adjust your air by using a gentler, downward stream for low notes and a smaller, faster, more focused stream for high notes. Here, the lower D♭ and higher D♭ use the same fingering.

Remember, each note comes with a fingering diagram showing you which keys to press.
   - Black circles mean press this key down.
   - White and Gray circles mean don't press this key.

Scan the QR Code

to Listen to the scale!

D♭ Major Scale (Down)

Here is the D♭ major scale descending. The scale begins on the higher D♭ note and every new note goes lower in sound. For the D♭ major scale descending we will play the notes D♭, C, B♭, A♭, G♭, F, E♭, then back to D♭, only lower.

For beginners, playing full scales can take time. Some of the lowest and highest notes need more practice, and that is perfectly fine. Play the notes you can, learn them at your own pace, and grow into the rest as you continue.

Many lower and higher notes on the piccolo use the same fingering. To reach the lower or higher sound, adjust your air by using a gentler, downward stream for low notes and a smaller, faster, more focused stream for high notes. Here, the lower D♭ and higher D♭ use the same fingering.

Remember, each note comes with a fingering diagram showing you which keys to press.
- Black circles mean press this key down.
- White and Gray circles mean don't press this key.

Scan the QR Code

to Listen to the scale!

A♭ Major Scale (Up)

This is the A♭ major scale ascending. The scale begins on the A♭ note and moves higher in sound with each new note. The A♭ major scale includes the notes A♭, B♭, C, D♭, E♭, F, and G.

For beginners, playing full scales can take time. Some of the lowest and highest notes need more practice, and that is perfectly fine. Play the notes you can, learn them at your own pace, and grow into the rest as you continue.

Many lower and higher notes on the piccolo use the same fingering. To reach the lower or higher sound, adjust your air by using a gentler, downward stream for low notes and a smaller, faster, more focused stream for high notes. Here, the lower A♭ and higher A♭ use the same fingering. Try it!

Remember, each note comes with a fingering diagram showing you which keys to press.
- Black circles mean press this key down.
- White and Gray circles mean don't press this key.

Scan the QR Code

to Listen to the scale!

A♭ Major Scale (Down)

Here is the A♭ major scale descending. The scale begins on the higher A♭ note and every new note goes lower in sound. For the A♭ major scale descending we will play the notes A♭, G, F, E♭, D♭, C, B♭, then back to A♭, only lower.

For beginners, playing full scales can take time. Some of the lowest and highest notes need more practice, and that is perfectly fine. Play the notes you can, learn them at your own pace, and grow into the rest as you continue.

Many lower and higher notes on the piccolo use the same fingering. To reach the lower or higher sound, adjust your air by using a gentler, downward stream for low notes and a smaller, faster, more focused stream for high notes. Here, the lower A♭ and higher A♭ use the same fingering. Try it!

Remember, each note comes with a fingering diagram showing you which keys to press.
  - Black circles mean press this key down.
  - White and Gray circles mean don't press this key.

Scan the QR Code

to Listen to the scale!

A Major Scale (Up)

This is the A major scale ascending. The scale begins on the A note and moves higher in sound with each new note. The A major scale includes the notes A, B, C#, D, E, F#, and G#.

For beginners, playing full scales can take time. Some of the lowest and highest notes need more practice, and that is perfectly fine. Play the notes you can, learn them at your own pace, and grow into the rest as you continue.

Many lower and higher notes on the piccolo use the same fingering. To reach the lower or higher sound, adjust your air by using a gentler, downward stream for low notes and a smaller, faster, more focused stream for high notes. Here, the lower A and higher A use the same fingering. Try it!

Remember, each note comes with a fingering diagram showing you which keys to press.
  - Black circles mean press this key down.
  - White and Gray circles mean don't press this key.

Scan the QR Code

to Listen to the scale!

A Major Scale (Down)

Here is the A major scale descending. The scale begins on the higher A note and every new note goes lower in sound. For the A major scale descending we will play the notes A, G#, F#, E, D, C#, B, then back to A, only lower.

For beginners, playing full scales can take time. Some of the lowest and highest notes need more practice, and that is perfectly fine. Play the notes you can, learn them at your own pace, and grow into the rest as you continue.

Many lower and higher notes on the piccolo use the same fingering. To reach the lower or higher sound, adjust your air by using a gentler, downward stream for low notes and a smaller, faster, more focused stream for high notes. Here, the lower A and higher A use the same fingering. Try it!

Remember, each note comes with a fingering diagram showing you which keys to press.
  - Black circles mean press this key down.
  - White and Gray circles mean don't press this key.

Scan the QR Code

to Listen to the scale!

G♭ Major Scale (Up)

This is the G♭ major scale ascending. The scale begins on the G♭ note and moves higher in sound with each new note. The G♭ major scale includes the notes G♭, A♭, B♭, C♭ (C♭ is the same as B), D♭, E♭, and F.

In music, some notes can have two different names even though they sound exactly the same. This is called being enharmonic. C♭ (C flat) and B are one of these pairs.

When you see C♭, it means play one half step lower than C. When you move one half step lower from C, you land on B. So even though they look different on paper, C♭ and B sound the same when you play them.

Remember, each note comes with a fingering diagram showing you which keys to press.
- Black circles mean press this key down.
- White and Gray circles mean don't press this key.

Scan the QR Code

to Listen to the scale!

G♭ Major Scale (Down)

Here is the G♭ major scale descending. The scale begins on the higher G♭ note and every new note goes lower in sound. For the G♭ major scale descending we will play the notes G♭, F, E♭, D♭, C♭ (B), B♭, A♭, then back to G♭, only lower.

For beginners, playing full scales can take time. Some of the lowest and highest notes need more practice, and that is perfectly fine. Play the notes you can, learn them at your own pace, and grow into the rest as you continue.

Many lower and higher notes on the piccolo use the same fingering. To reach the lower or higher sound, adjust your air by using a gentler, downward stream for low notes and a smaller, faster, more focused stream for high notes. Here, the lower G♭ and higher G♭ use the same fingering. Try it!

Remember, each note comes with a fingering diagram showing you which keys to press.
- Black circles mean press this key down.
- White and Gray circles mean don't press this key.

Scan the QR Code

to Listen to the scale!

Mary Had a Little Lamb

Lowell Mason (1831)

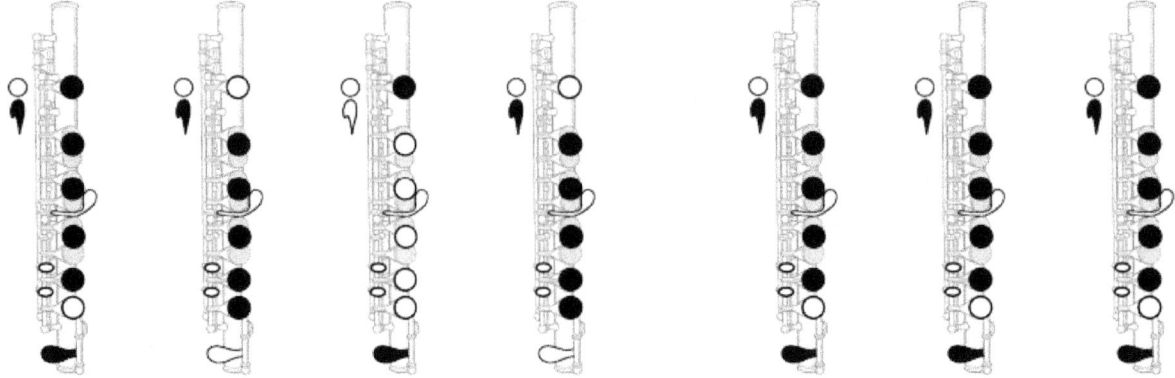

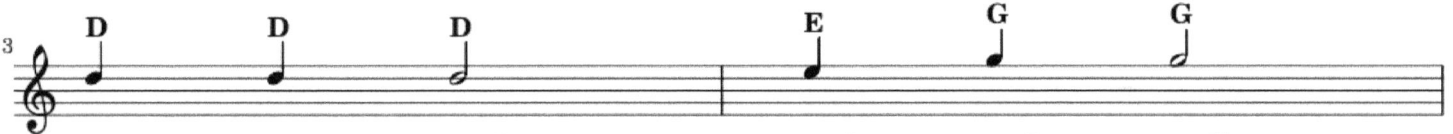

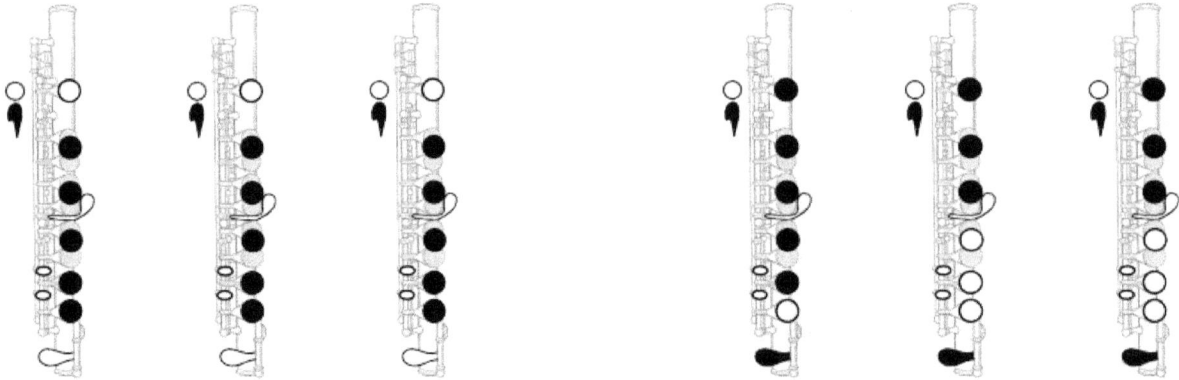

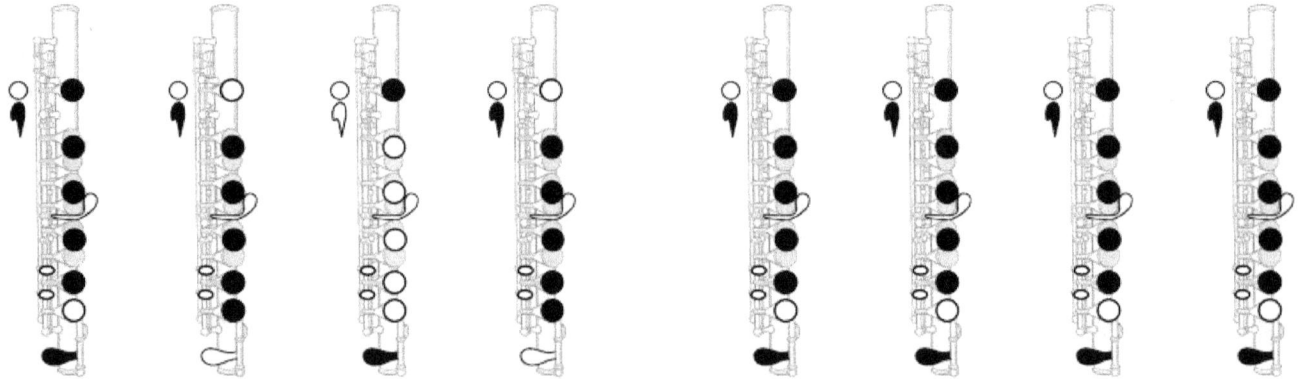

The Legend of Mary and Her Lamb

As the legend goes, this song was inspired by an actual event involving a girl named Mary Elizabeth Sawyer (1806–1889), who lived in Sterling, Massachusetts. According to Mary's writings, when she was a young girl, she nursed a sickly lamb back to health, and the lamb became attached to her. One day, the lamb followed Mary to school, creating a scene that amused her classmates and teacher.

Today, the Redstone Schoolhouse, where Mary's lamb supposedly followed her, is preserved as a historical site in Sudbury, Massachusetts, and continues to commemorate the tale.

Scan the QR Code

to Listen to the song!

Twinkle Twinkle Little Star

Traditional (1806)

Scan the
QR Code

to Listen to
the song!

Frère Jacques (Brother John)

Traditional French (18th Century)

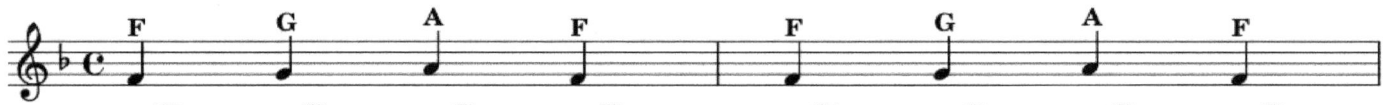

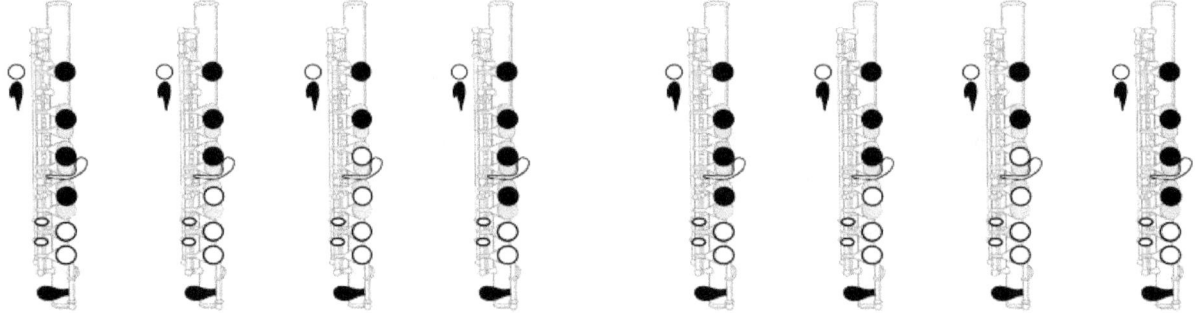

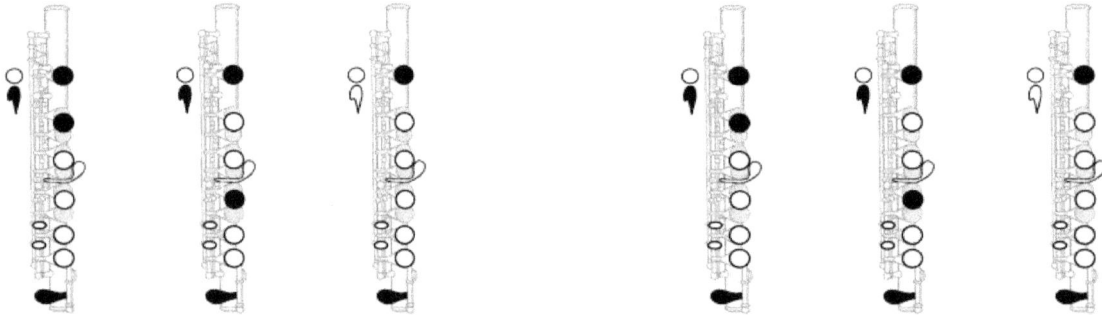

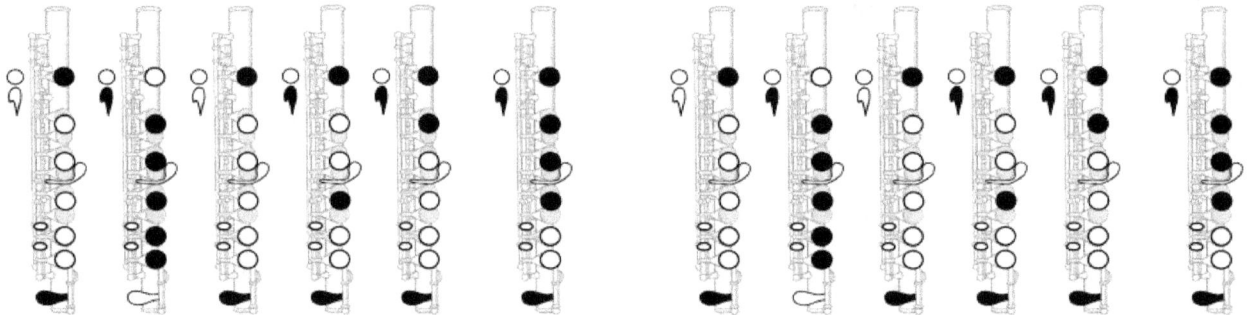

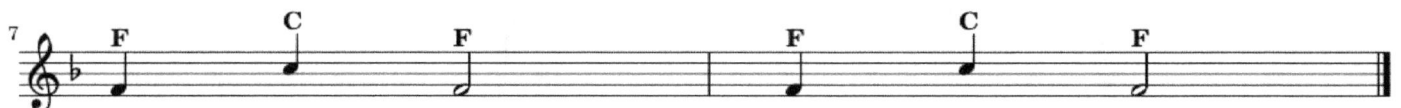

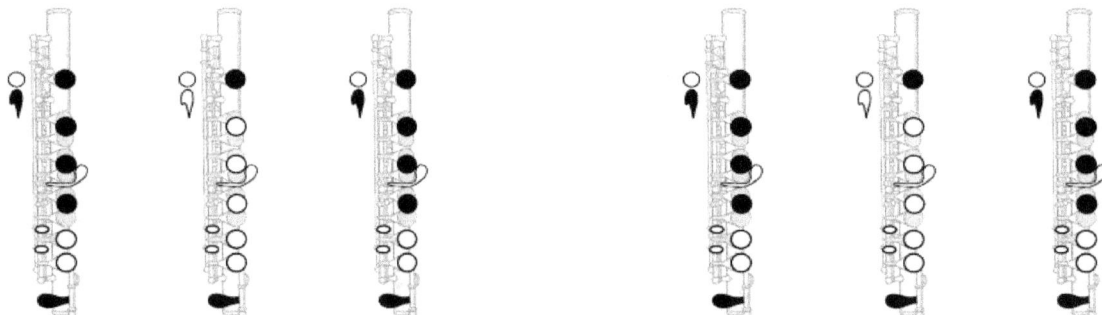

Scan the QR Code

to Listen to the song!

Pop Goes the Weasel

Traditional English (c1850)

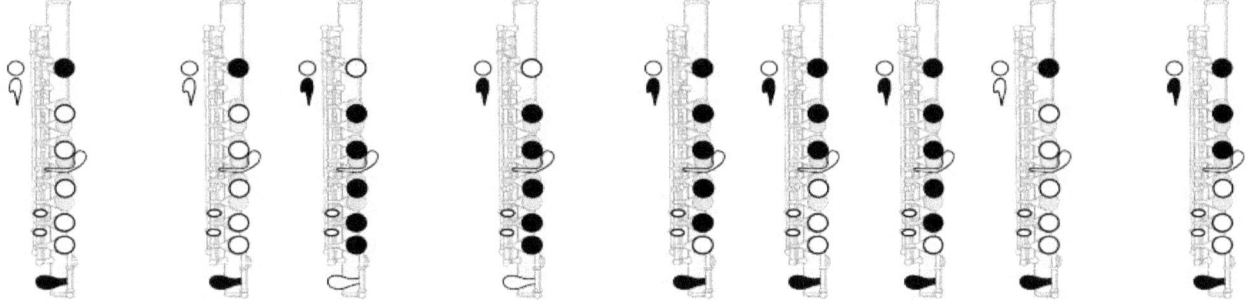

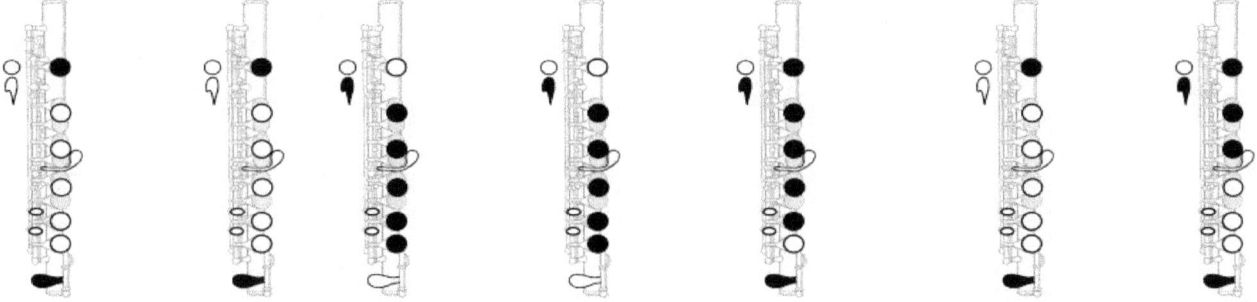

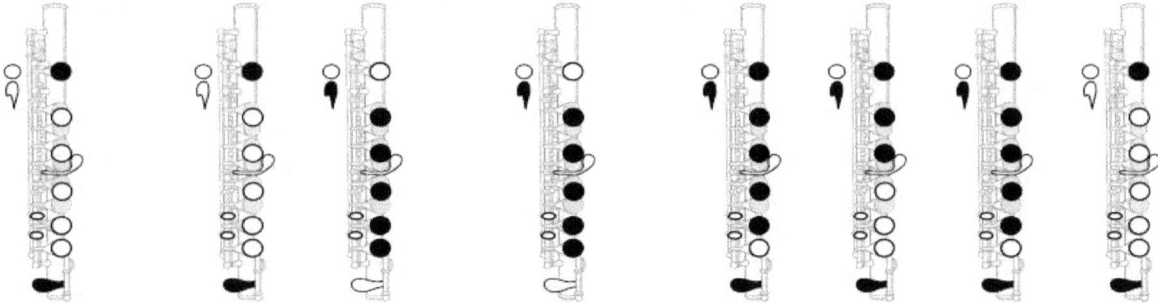

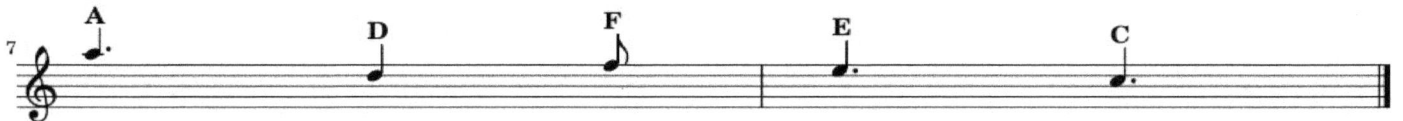

Scan the QR Code

to Listen to the song!

Ring Around the Rosie

Traditional English (19th Century)

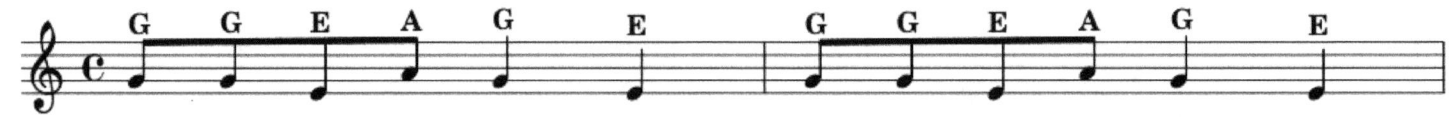

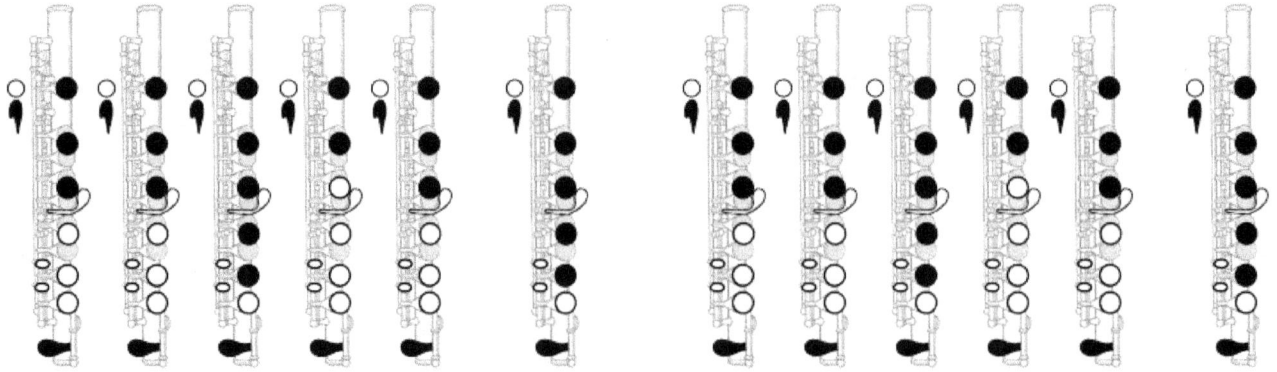

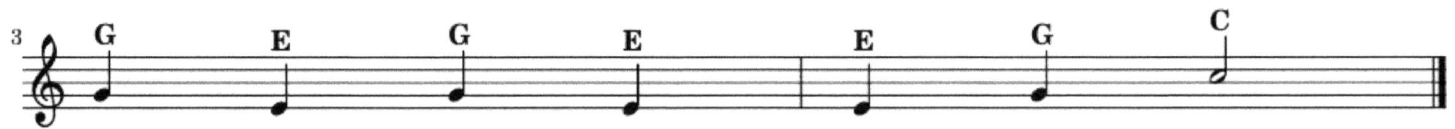

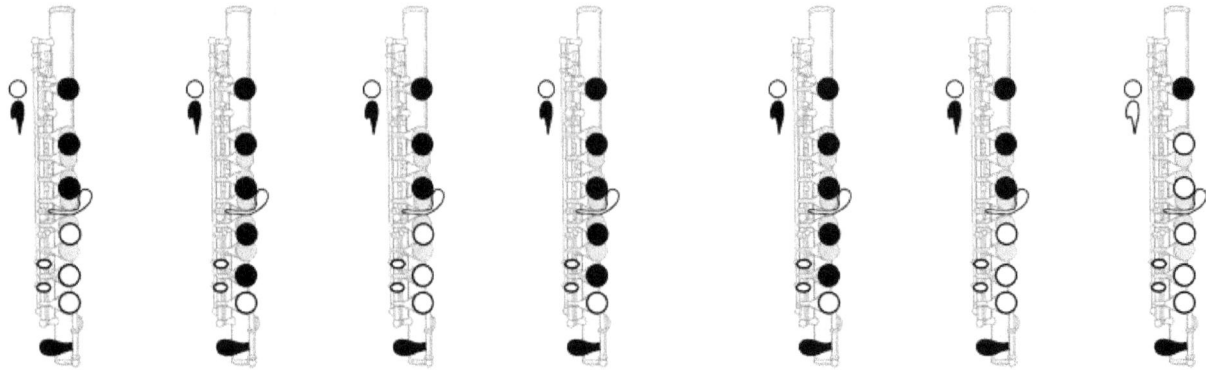

Row Row Row Your Boat

Traditional American (19th Century)

Scan the QR Code

to Listen to the song!

This Old Man

Traditional English (19th Century)

Scan the QR Code to Listen to the song!

London Bridge is Falling Down

Traditional English (18th Century)

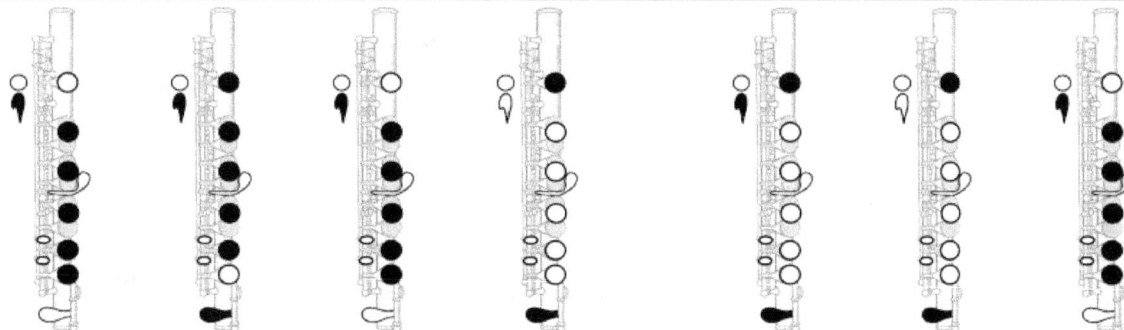

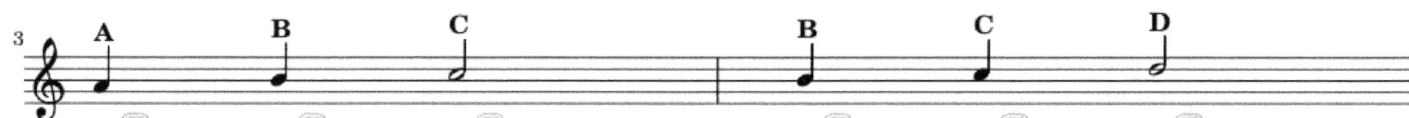

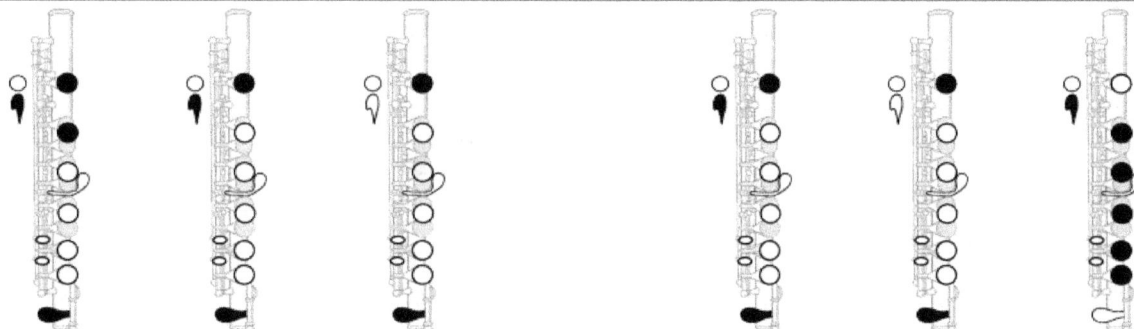

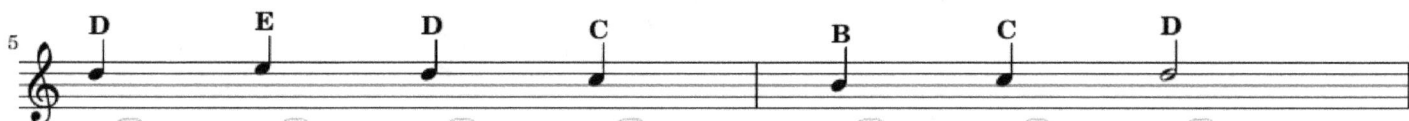

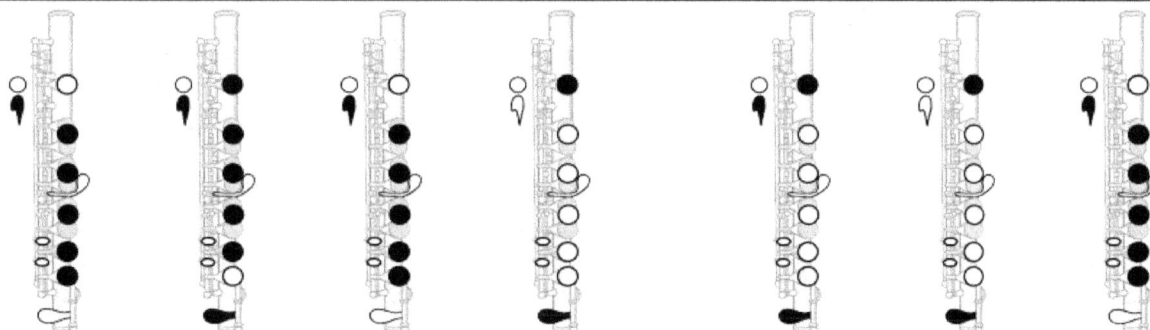

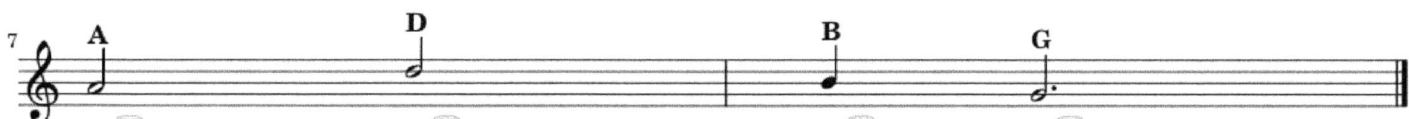

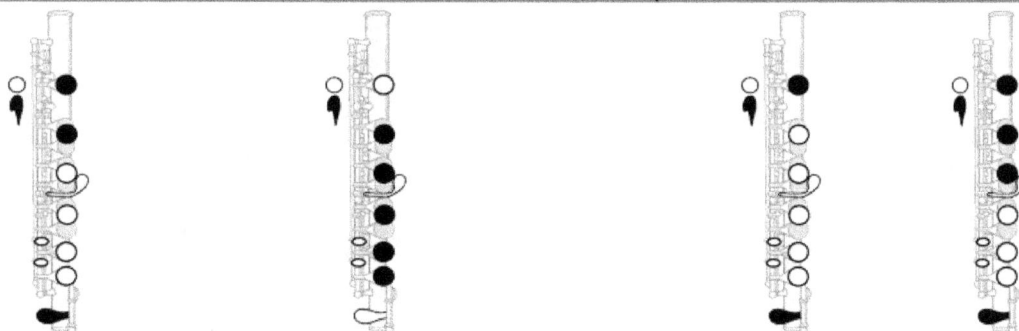

Scan the QR Code to Listen to the song!

It's a Jazzy Day!

Martin Freres (2025)

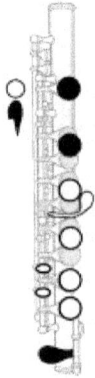

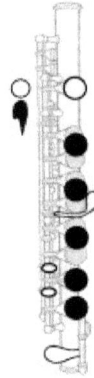

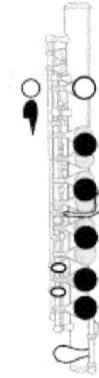

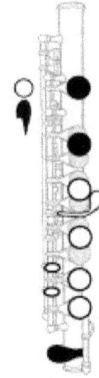

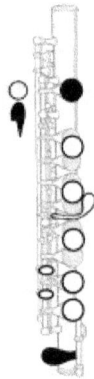

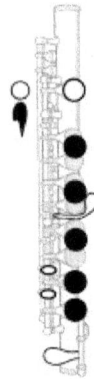

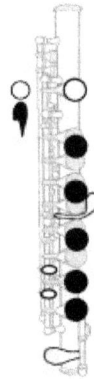

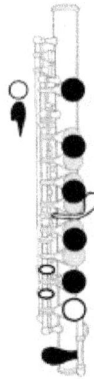

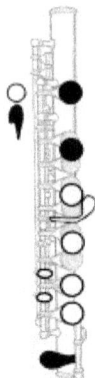

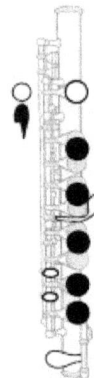

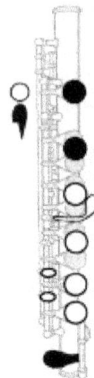

It's a Jazzy Day!

This tune plays low notes and then jumps an octave higher. An **octave** is when a note is played again at a higher or lower pitch, but is still the same note. In this song, that happens with the lower and higher A note.

IT'S A JAZZY DAY

Scan the QR Code

to Listen to the song!

Camptown Races

Stephen Foster (1850)

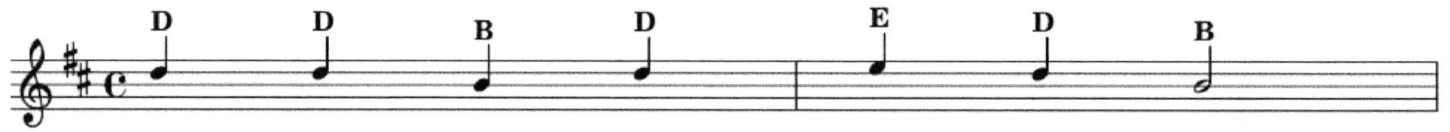

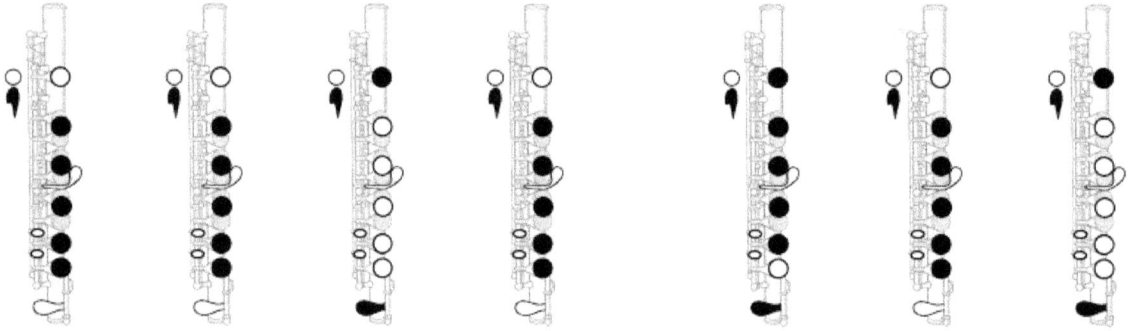

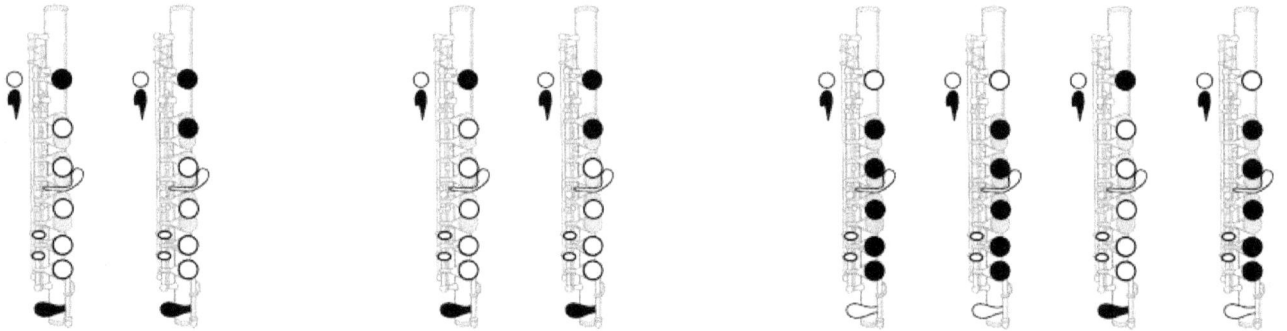

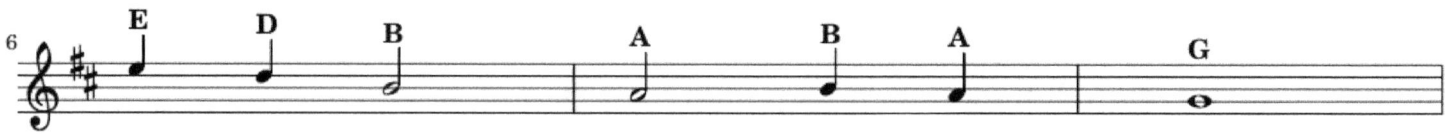

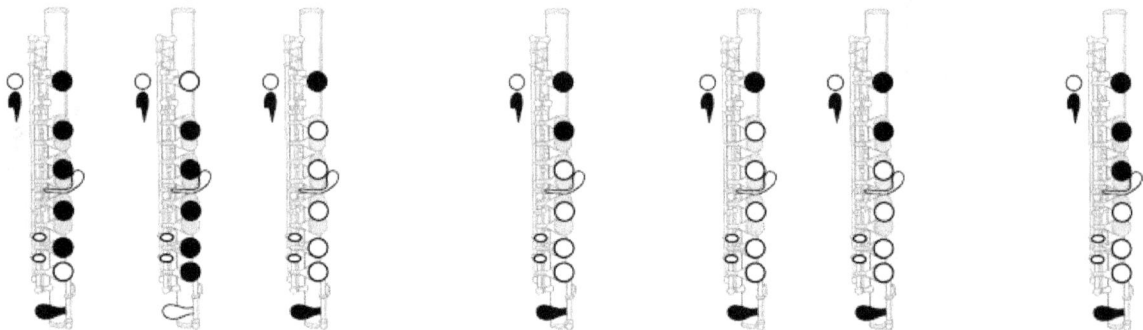

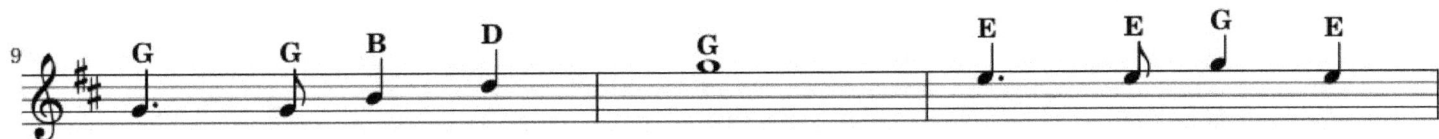

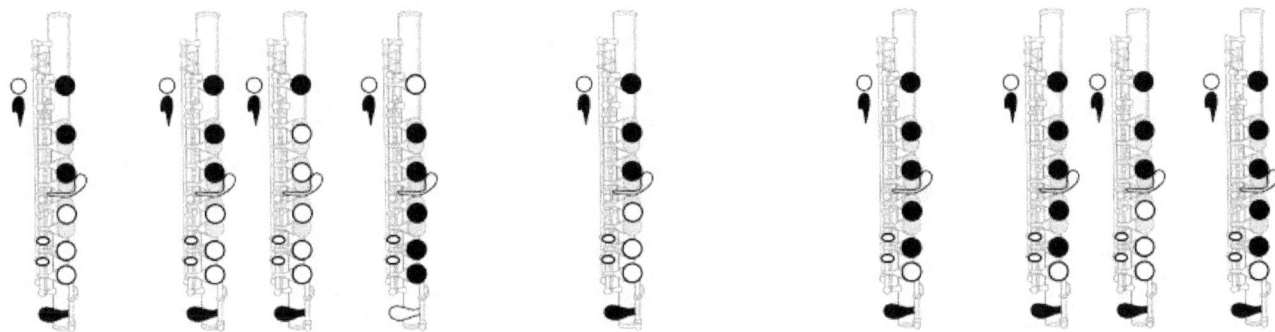

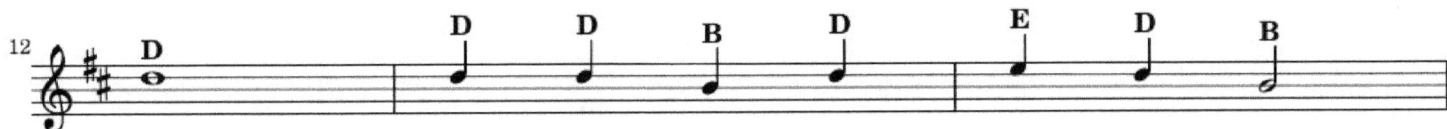

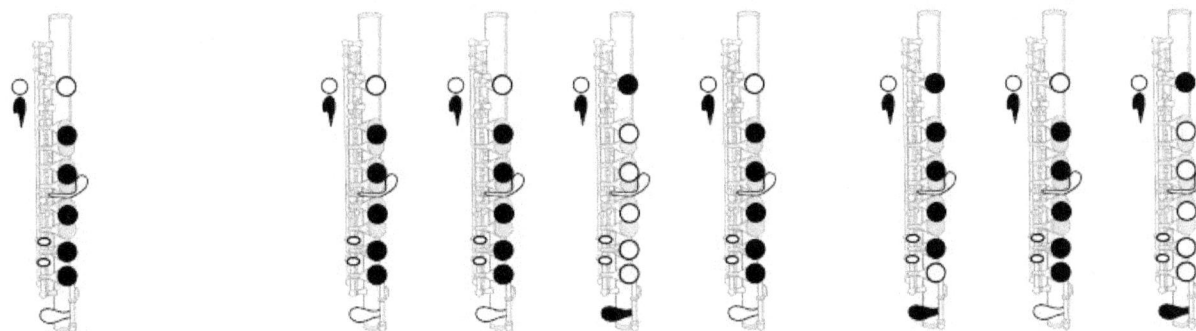

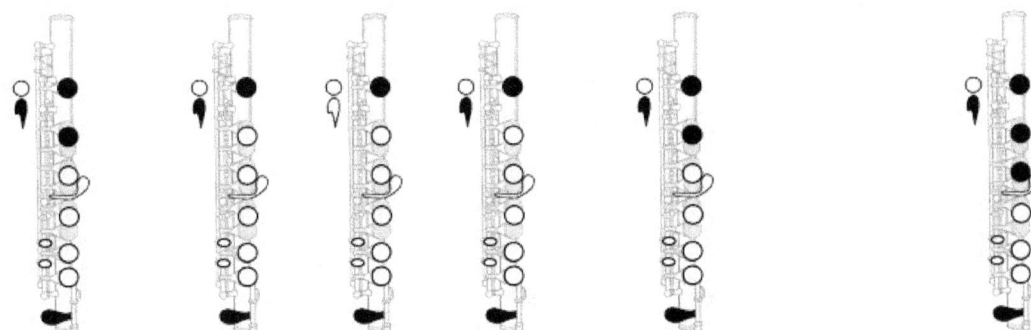

Stephen C. Foster (1826–1864)

Known as the "Father of American Music," Stephen Foster wrote songs that became part of America's cultural history. Born in Pennsylvania on July 4, 1826, he composed beloved tunes such as *Camptown Races, Oh! Susanna,* and *That's What's the Matter*, all featured in this book. His music remains timeless, simple, and memorable, ideal for learning melody, rhythm, and phrasing.

Scan the QR Code

to Listen to the song!

Oh! Susanna

Stephen Foster (1848)

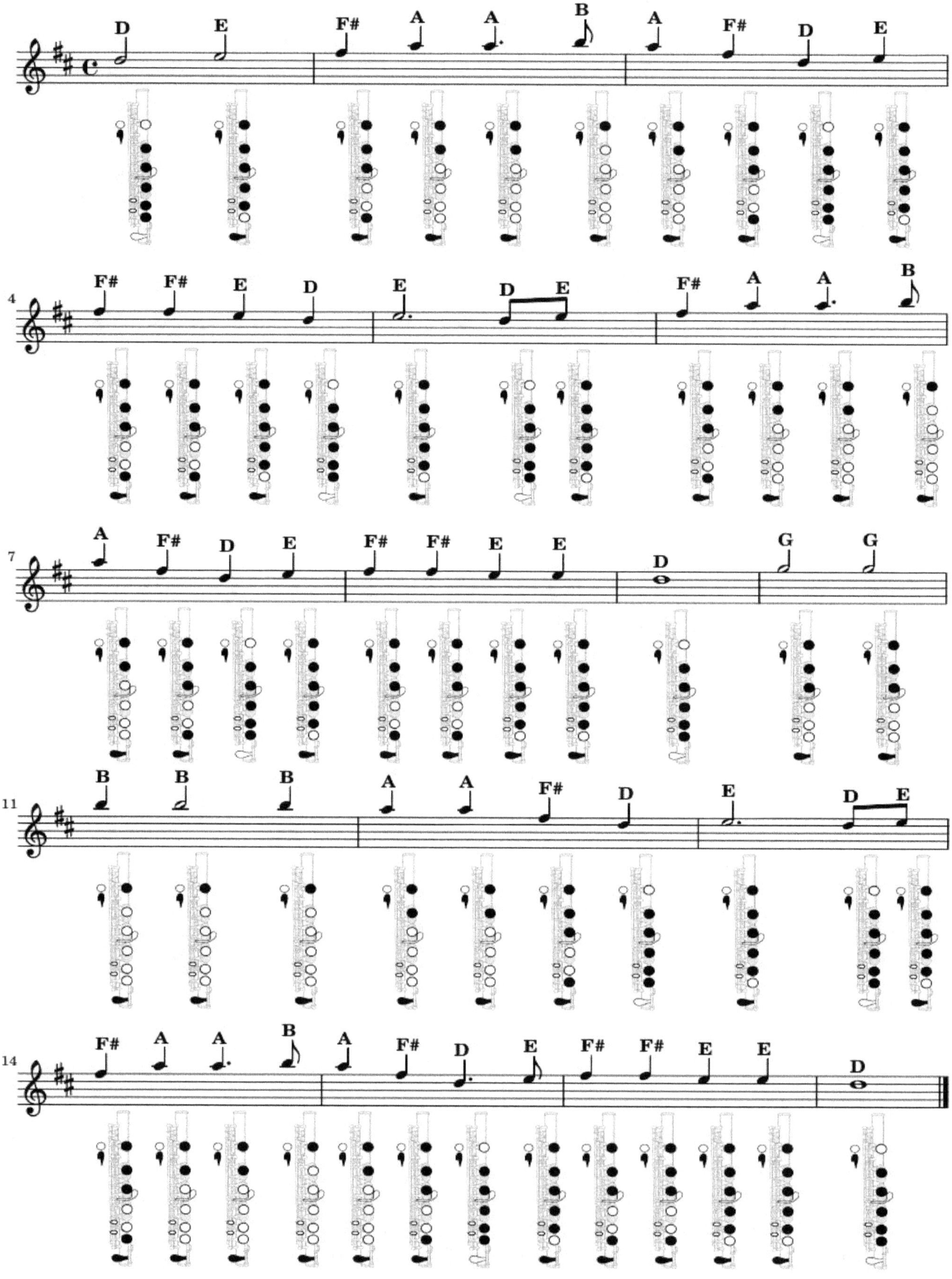

Scan the QR Code to Listen to the song!

That's What's the Matter

Stephen Foster (1862)

Scan the QR Code

to Listen to the song!

Ode to Joy

Ludwig van Beethoven (1824)

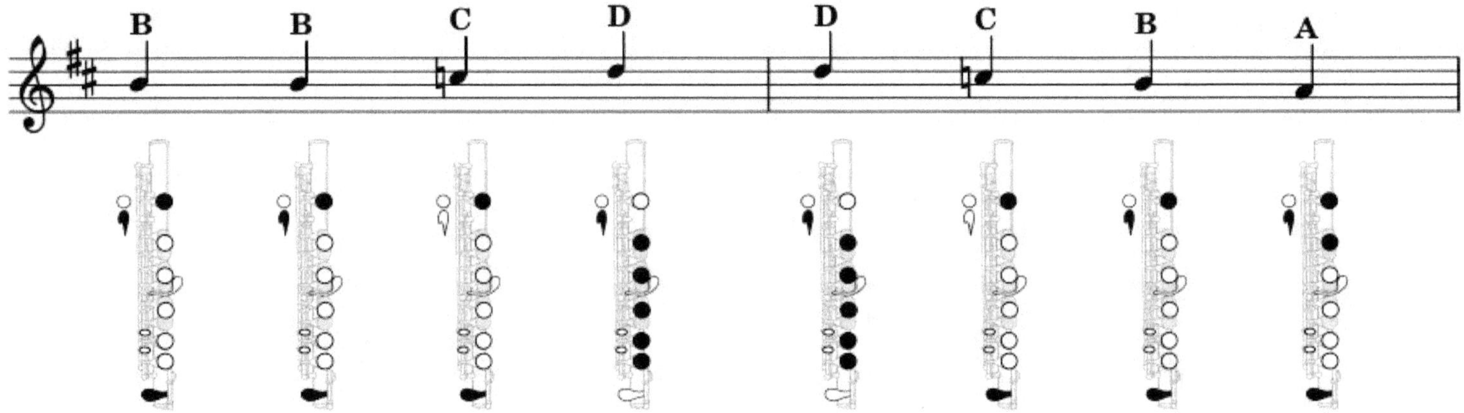

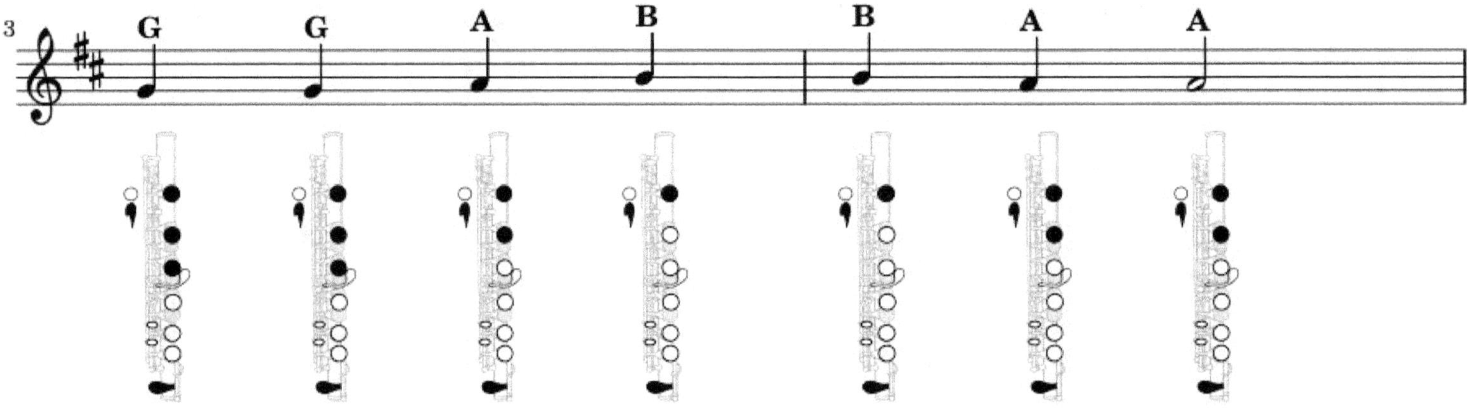

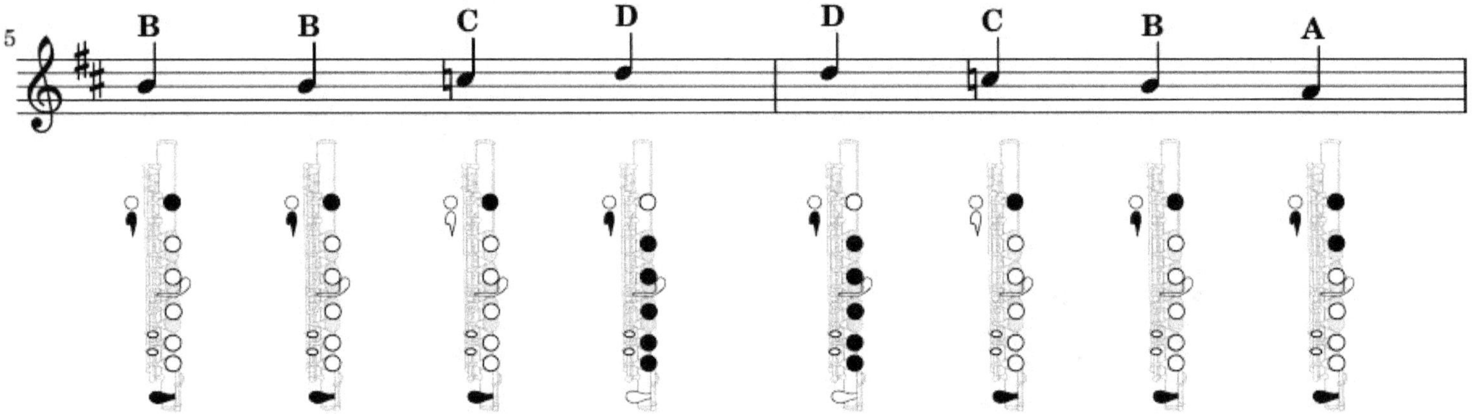

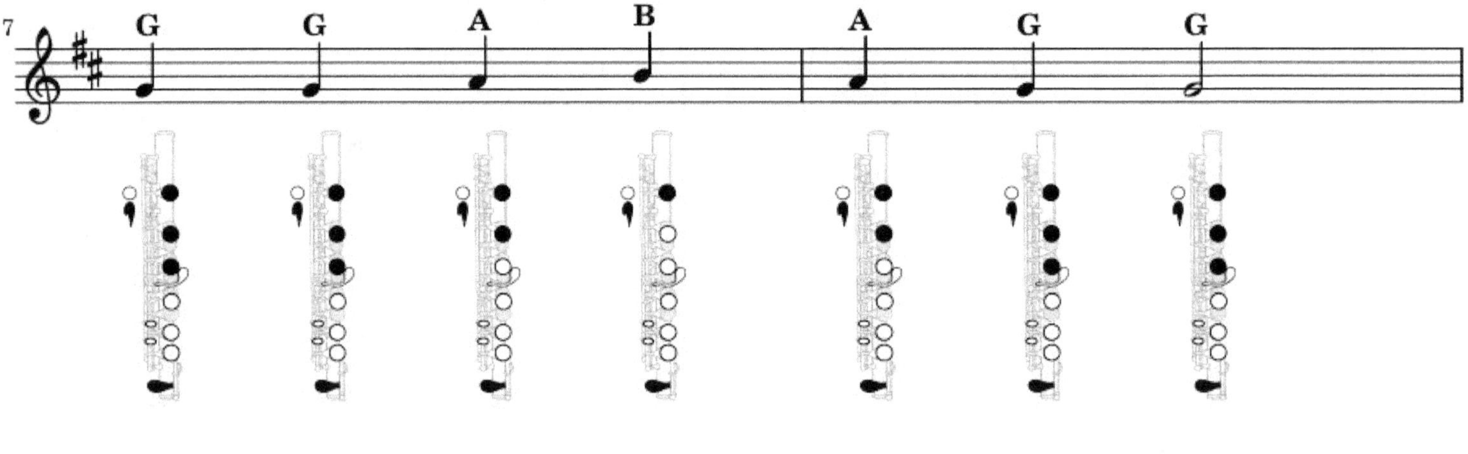

Scan the QR Code to Listen to the song!

She'll Be Comin' 'Round the Mountain

Traditional American (19th Century)

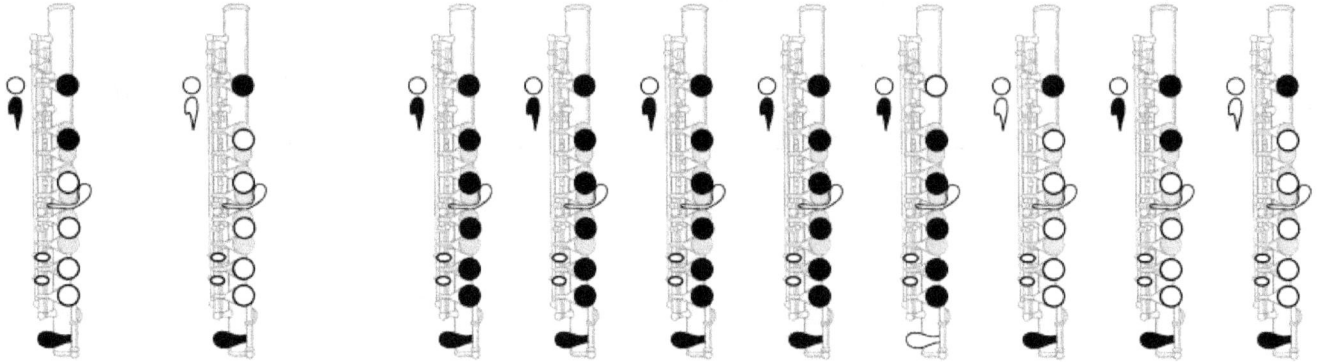

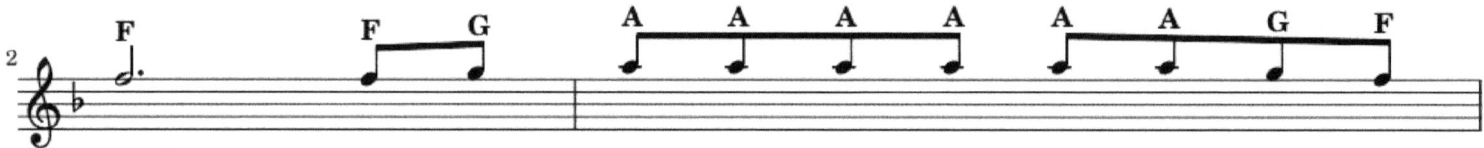

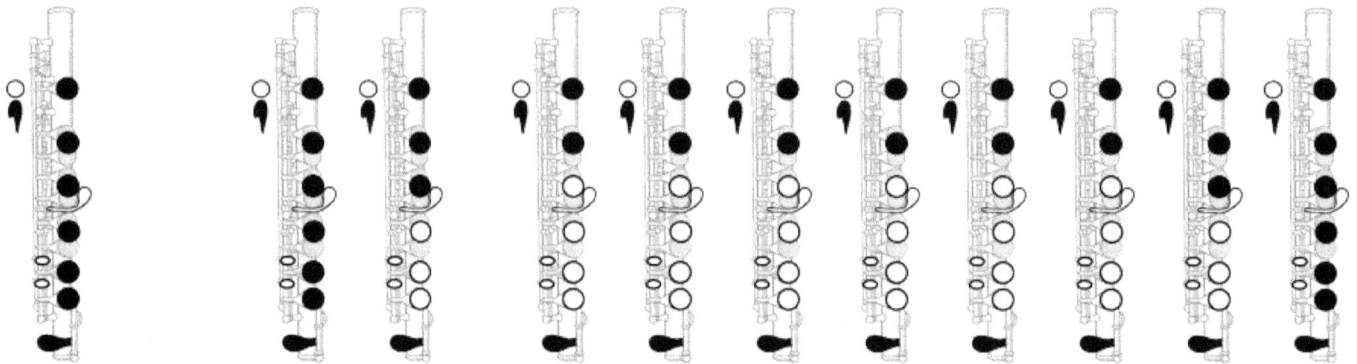

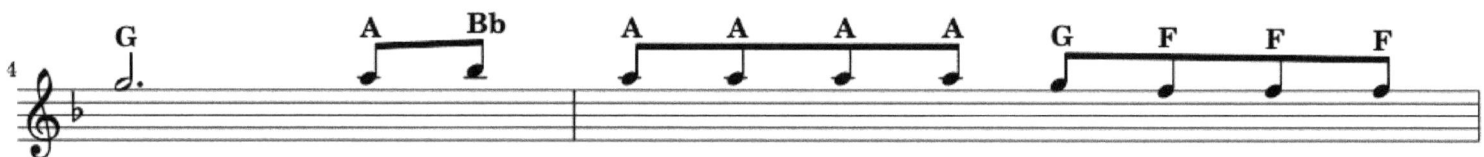

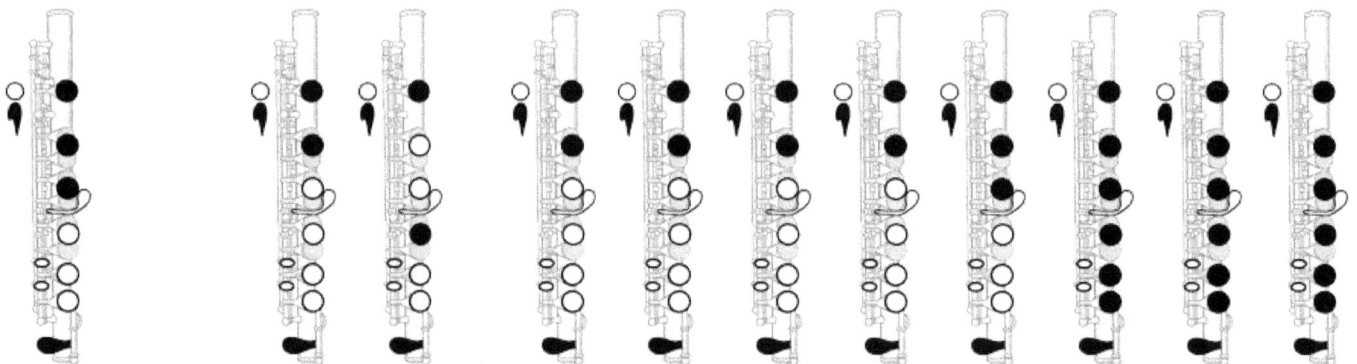

Scan the QR Code

to Listen to the song!

When the Saints Go Marching In

Traditional American (19th Century)

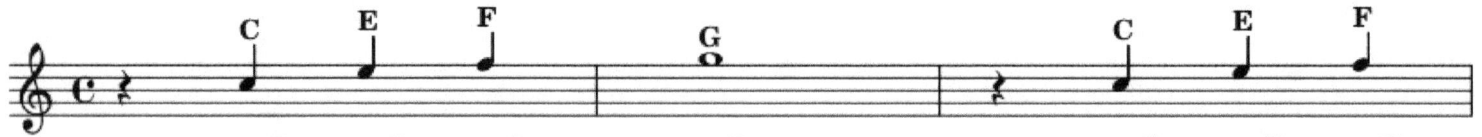

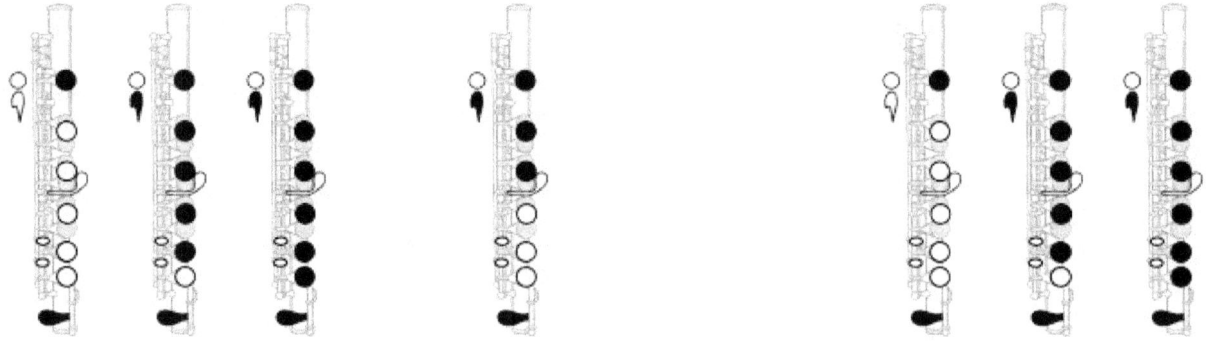

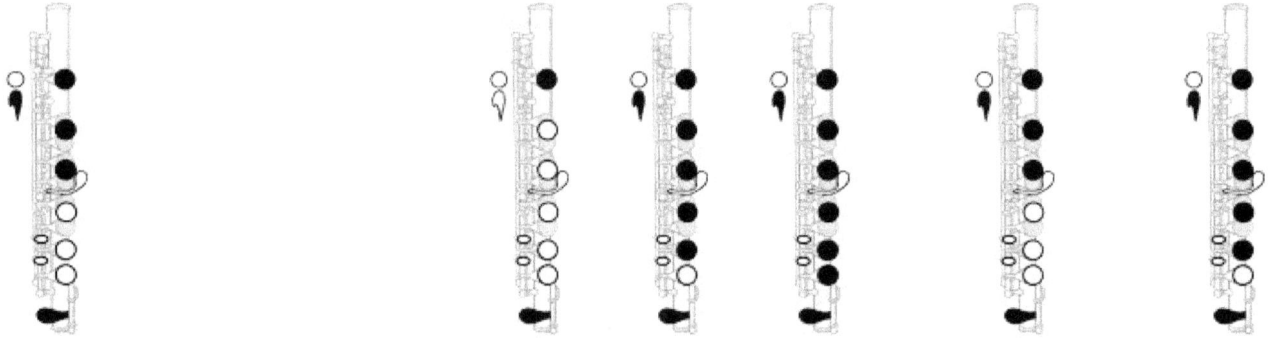

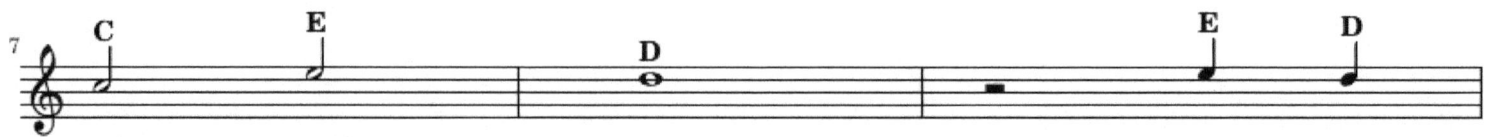

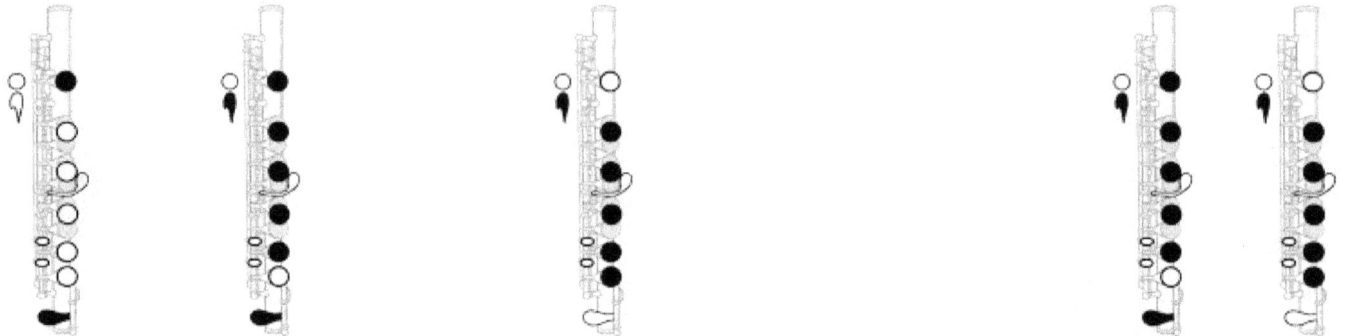

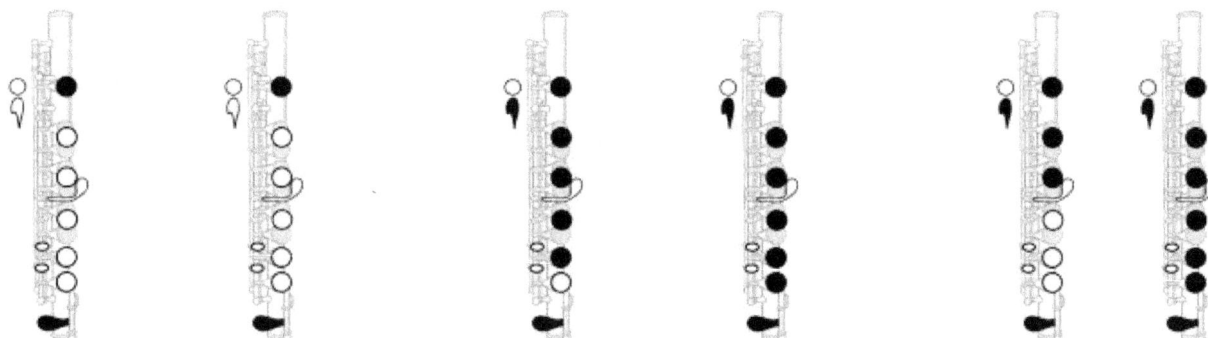

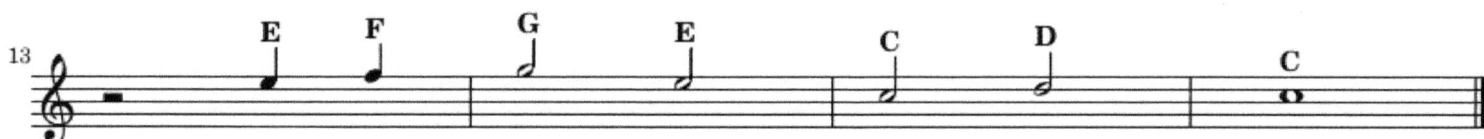

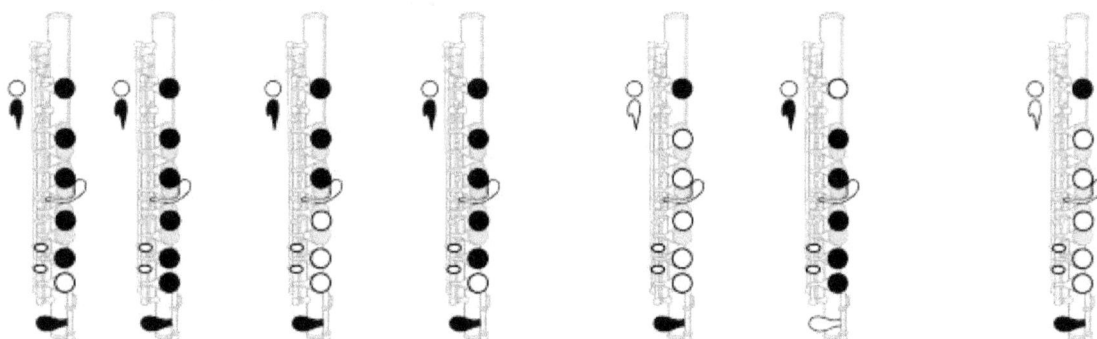

Amazing Grace

William Walker (1835)

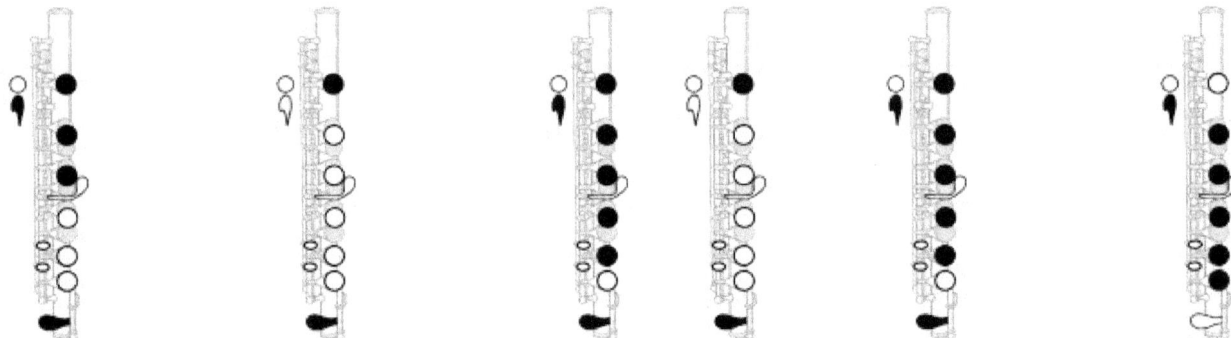

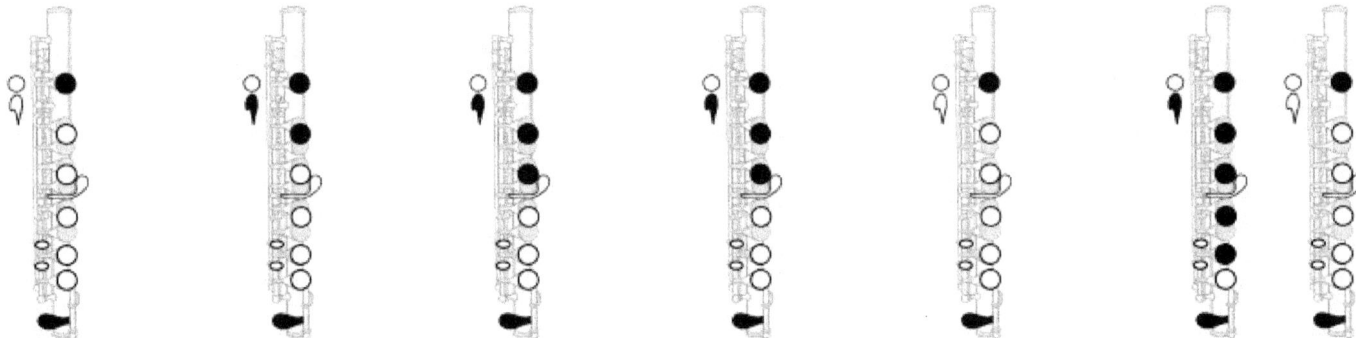

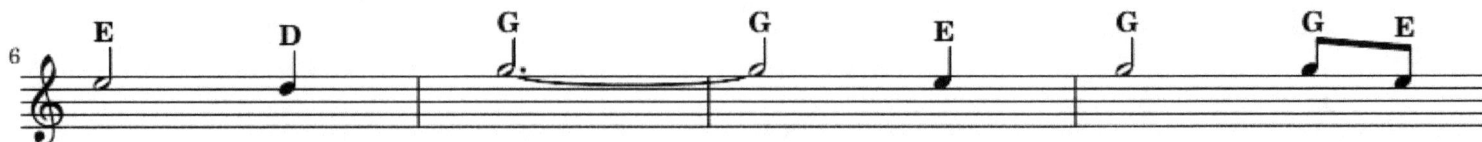

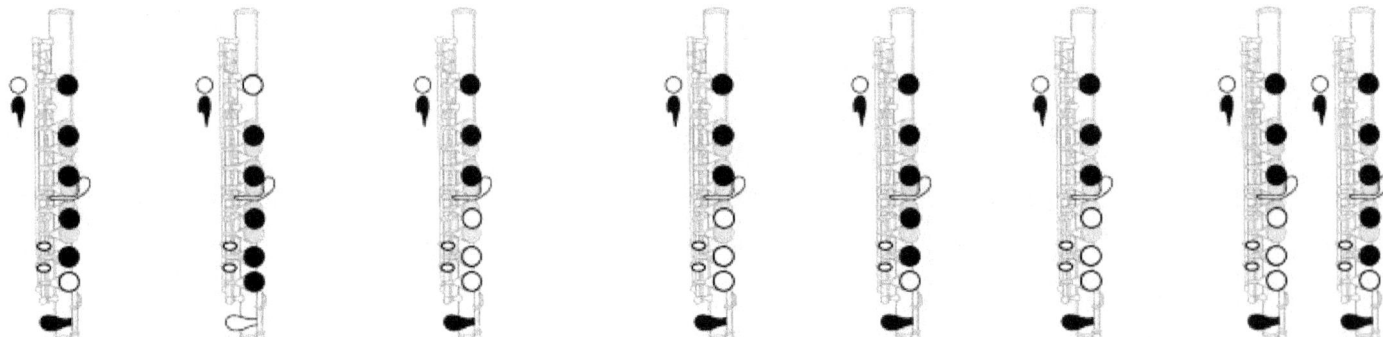

Musical History of "Amazing Grace"

The tune we use for *Amazing Grace* is an early American melody called *New Britain*. It's an old American melody that first appeared in a music book in 1829.

In 1835, a musician named William Walker arranged the *Amazing Grace* words with the *New Britain* melody in his book *Southern Harmony*. The two fit so well that the pairing quickly became popular all over the world. The rest is history!

Scan the QR Code

to Listen to the song!

Jingle Bells

J. Pierpont (1857)

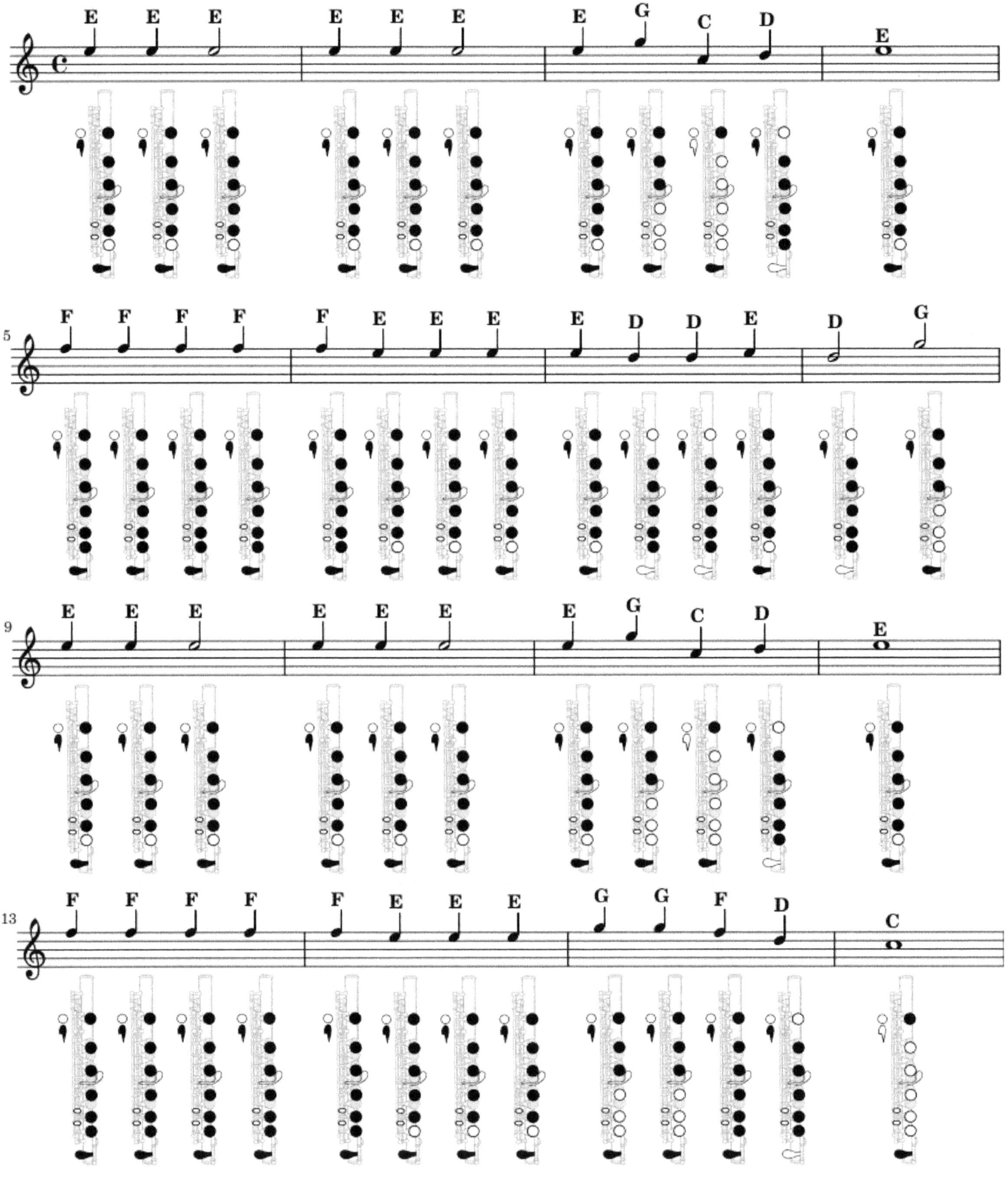

Scan the QR Code to Listen to the song!

Up On the Housetop

Benjamin Hanby (1864)

Piccolo Fingering Chart

The Piccolo Fingering Chart begins with the note D4. Next, the chart rises step by step, showing flats (♭) and sharps (#), all the way up to C7. This fingering chart is presented as a chromatic scale.

A **Chromatic Scale** is a musical scale that goes up or down by half steps, the smallest steps in music. Think of playing every single note in order, without skipping any. Scan the QR code to listen to the whole scale from D4 to C7.

D4 to B4

Piccolo Fingering Chart

The numbers next to the notes, like 4, 5, and 6, are called octave numbers. Octave numbers are the numbers you see next to a note name, like D4 or F5. They tell you how high or low a note sounds on your instrument or in music. Each time you go to the next higher sounding C note, you move up one octave and the number increases by one. So, the number helps show which version of the note you're playing: low, middle, or high.

C5 to B5

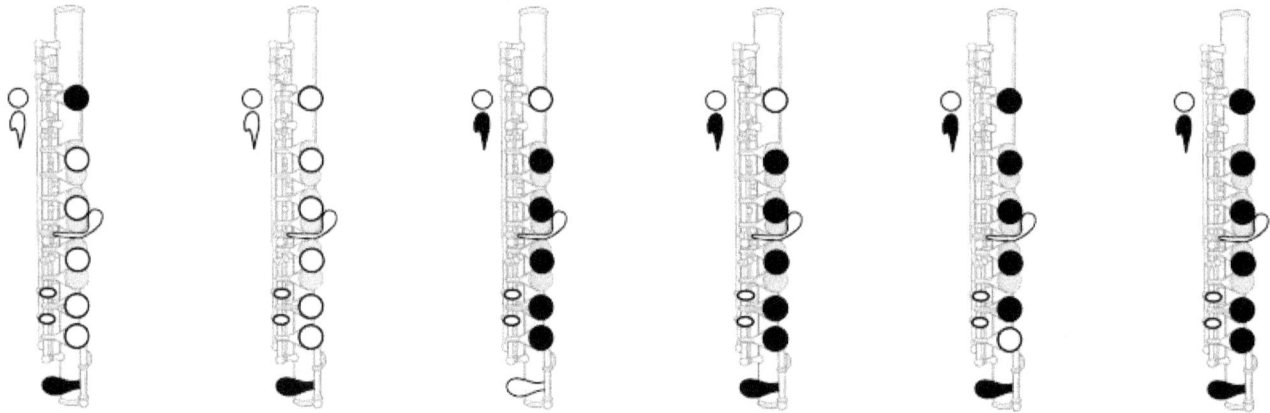

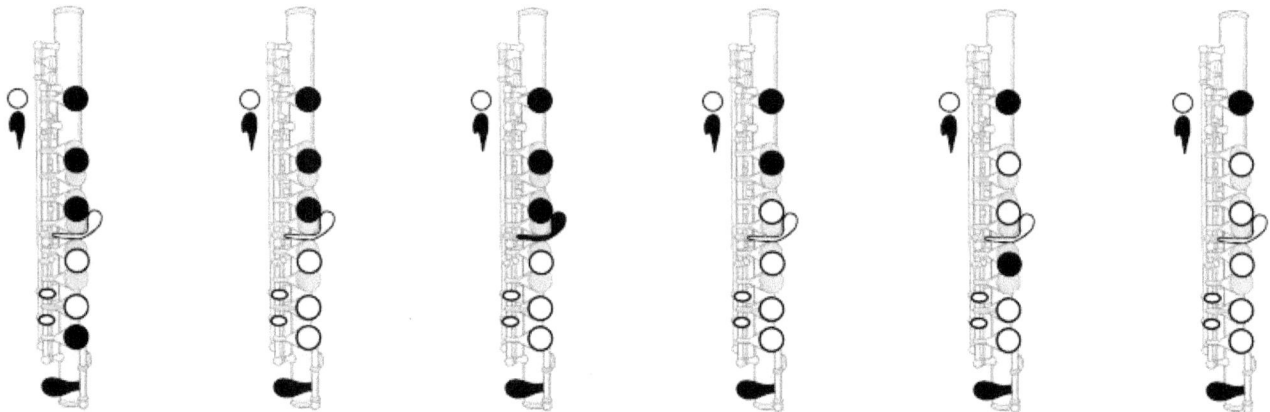

Piccolo Fingering Chart

C6 to C7

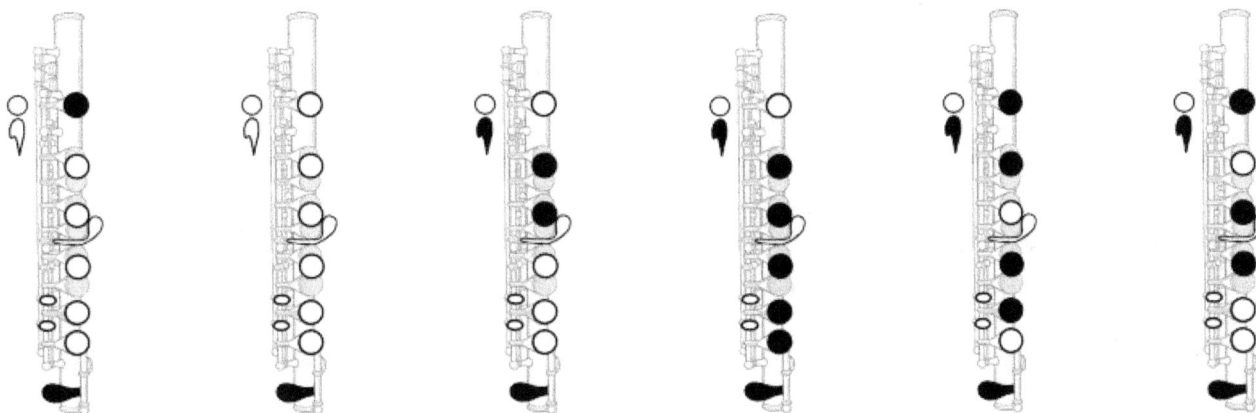

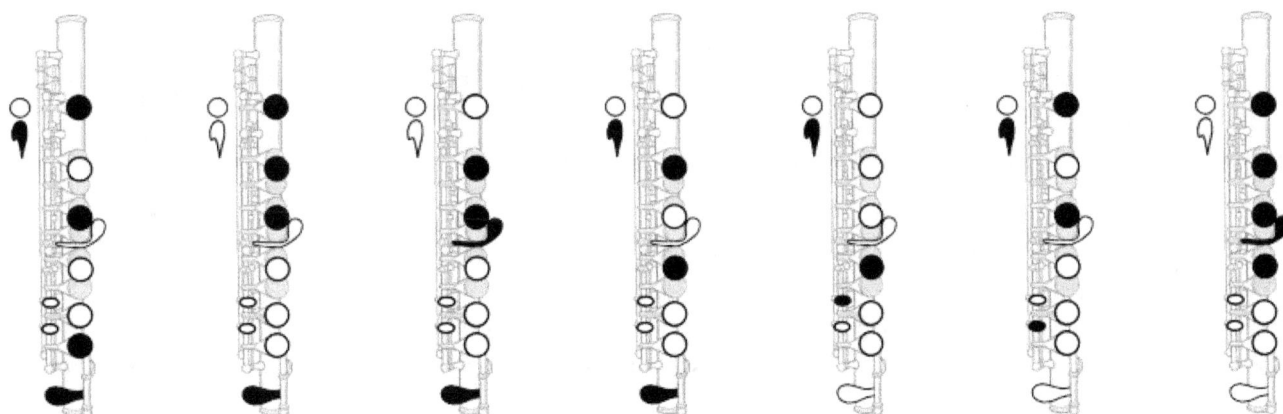

Scan the
QR Code

to Listen to
the scale!

History of the Piccolo

The piccolo is one of the oldest musical ideas in the world. It is a small instrument that makes sound by blowing air across a hole. Long before the modern piccolo existed, people around the world made small, high-pitched flutes from natural materials such as bone, wood, and ivory.

Some of the earliest flutes ever discovered date back more than 40,000 years. These ancient instruments were found in caves and were made from animal bones or ivory. Many had only a few finger holes and produced bright, piercing sounds, similar to the sound of today's piccolo.

As civilizations developed, small flutes became more common. Ancient Egyptian, Greek, Chinese, and Native American cultures all created short flutes designed to play higher notes. In Medieval Europe, a simple wooden flute called the fife became popular. The fife is an early ancestor of the piccolo and was often used outdoors because its sound could travel long distances.

During the Renaissance and Baroque periods, small flutes continued to evolve. Instrument makers refined their shapes, adjusted finger hole placement, and worked to improve tuning. These early piccolos and fifes were usually made from a single piece of wood and had no keys, which limited the notes they could play comfortably.

In the 1700s, French instrument maker Jacques Martin Hotteterre helped standardize flute design by separating the instrument into three parts and improving tuning and finger placement. These enhancements influenced both the flute and the smaller instruments that would later become the modern piccolo.

Major changes came in the 1800s, when Theobald Boehm redesigned the flute's key system and tone hole placement. His ideas were later adapted for the piccolo, leading to better tuning, easier fingerings, and a stronger, clearer sound. Metal tubing was introduced, making the piccolo more reliable and easier to play.

Today's piccolo is a small but powerful instrument. It is used in orchestras, bands, marching groups, and classrooms. Though much smaller than the flute, its bright sound allows it to rise above the music, continuing a tradition that began thousands of years ago.

Piccolo

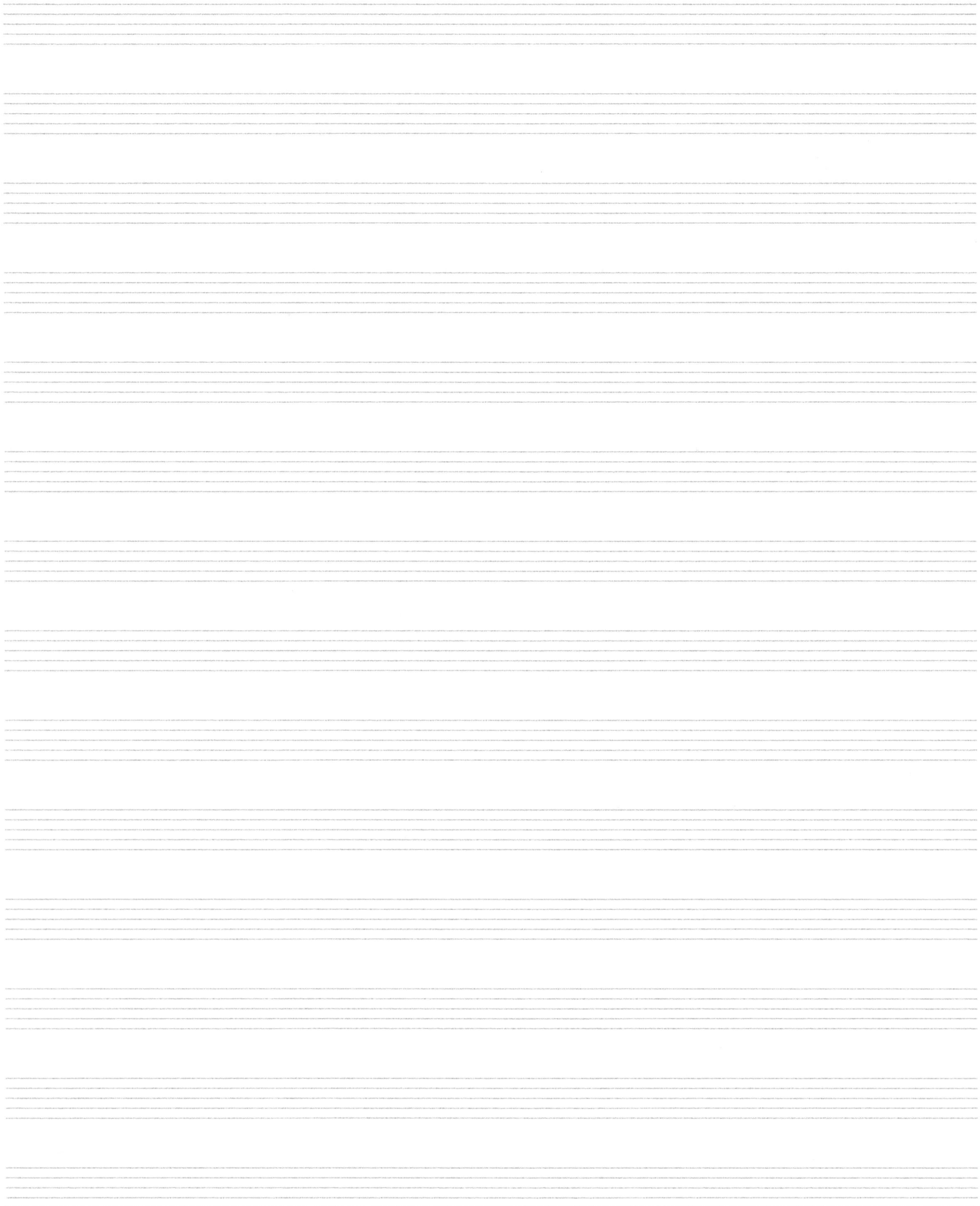

www.ingramcontent.com/pod-product-compliance
Lightning Source LLC
LaVergne TN
LVHW081336060426
835513LV00014B/1313